PETER MACGOWAN KEMP. T   uthful, but he is known to most   re foot nothing but a fiery charac   gladly. Prickly and tough on the outside, yet to those closest, soft on the inside. Once asked by a millionaire if he could build him a yacht, Peter replied, 'I can build it but can you bloody well sail it?' Peter is well known in yachting circles for his quest for accuracy – a virtue loved by designers and loathed by builders. He will tackle problems head on, saying, 'Don't just look at it, just do it'. Or, 'He who never made a mistake never made anything.' This quest for perfection almost drove him to self-destruction but the anchor of family and a love of the hills kept him on the straight and narrow. Peter left school at fourteen to start an apprenticeship in Harland and Wolff, then John Brown's. When work in the shipyards dried up, he moved into yacht building. He's now firmly on dry land as shop steward/staff council representative for all Sainsbury's branches in Scotland and Northern Ireland. At home Peter is a quiet, private, family man with many interests and talents, such as painting, poetry, photography, social and industrial history, ancestry research, and music. Above all he has a love of Scotland that kept him there, staying through hard times and good, unlike many others who left to search for a better life.

Of Big Hills and Wee Men

PETER KEMP

Luath Press Limited

EDINBURGH

www.luath.co.uk

First published 2004

The paper used in this book is recyclable.
It is made from low chlorine pulps produced in a low energy,
low emission manner from renewable forests.

Printed and bound by
Bell & Bain Ltd., Glasgow

Typeset in Sabon 10.5 pt

Contents

Acknowledgements

THIS BOOK IS A TRIBUTE TO my wife May and my sons, Tommy, Peter, Scott and Douglas, for their support. Also to my friends Bill MacKay, Irene Cook, Pat Wright, Susan Fyfe, John McEwan and Derek Sakol. To all of the members of the Glasgow HF and Gleniffer outdoor clubs. To the memory of a good friend Robert who died on the Cobbler, and the late Dan McPhee, Bobby Stirling and my father.

To the inspiration from the writings and poetry of Robert Burns, Robert Service, Patrick McGill, Samuel Coleridge Taylor, Dominic Behan, James Elroy Flecker, Hamish Henderson and Matt McGinn.

With a special thanks to Mary Brailey for her editorial help.

Lastly to John Tyrone Cuthill, James Kemp, Rab Doyle, Billy Billings and many, many others for their comradeship and company on the lang Scots miles we tramped together.

Last Man Standing

IT WAS NOW LATE SEPTEMBER. Forming a golden carpet, the last leaves were falling from the trees. As they say up here, the nights were fair drawing in. What summer we'd had was well and truly over and the cold grip of winter was not far away. Here I was making my way up onto the Kilpatrick Braes for the first time in over seven months, on old familiar tracks that in places were now well overgrown. Way back in February what had seemed to be the start of a promising year on the hills had fallen by the wayside when large parts of Britain were hit by foot and mouth outbreaks. Thousands of farm livestock were slaughtered and cremated in huge funeral pyres; huge swathes of countryside became no-go areas. Although Scotland north of the Clyde valley had remained clear, fear of the disease spreading north had put many areas of the country out of bounds for outdoor activities. The Kilpatrick hills, forming the southern edge of the Highlands, had been quiet for months, virtually abandoned by walkers – even I had ventured further afield. Now, after my enforced absence, I was sitting here on my own gazing fondly over a familiar but dreich and misty scene. I thought about that last and final visit to this spot with my late climbing partner of so many years, old Rab Doyle. Most of the old team had long since gone, ravaged by old age and ill health. Time had taken its toll and here I was virtually the last man still standing.

It was only just over a year ago that I lay here, eyes closed, feeling the pleasant glow from the weak sun overhead. Yet only minutes before, a fierce snow squall had passed over and if it wasn't for the sun's warmth you might easily have sworn that it was still winter. Beyond the shelter of the half-dead pine trees where we lay sunning ourselves, the bitterly cold wind would have cut you in two. But, yes, it most definitely was spring. The skylarks soared happily above us singing their little hearts out. Earlier on our way up the Humphreys Road a new lamb was born before our very eyes. Everywhere the daffodils were in full bloom.

Rab and I were taking our customary Sunday walk onto the Kilpatrick hills. Here, just inside the tree line out of the wind, we always stopped for a cup of hot tea before pressing up to the highest point of this escarpment called the Slacks. Below us, squeezed between the canal and railway in the morning mist, lay the sleepy hamlet of Old Kilpatrick, and the spindly Erskine Bridge spanning the Clyde in a wide graceful curve. Beyond where the river bends stood the former site of John Brown's shipyard, birthplace of many a famous ship, facing the mouth of the sun-sparkled River Cart. Before us in the bright spring sunshine lay the entire Clyde Valley, dominated by the vast sprawling mass of Glasgow, the dear green place. There was a time not too long ago when the old heavy industries would have made this view much less clear. But today we could see from the Cowal hills and Greenock in the west to the Pentlands in the east. And there, covered with light dustings of snow, were the Galloway hills to the south, bulky Ailsa Craig or 'Paddy's Milestone' looming off the Ayrshire coast in the shimmering waters of the Firth of Clyde, and the ragged peaks of the Arran hills poking up beyond the Renfrew hills of Misty Law. The view below us – apart from the modern housing, the bridge, the airport – might well have been the same over a century ago. Except that this once busy river was now dead: not a single ship in sight, not even the old paddle steamer the Waverley, nor the old sewage boats the Dalmarnock and the Garroch Head – both now operating off West Africa as water carriers. God, what a thought.

As we loafed about, lazy, contemplating the view, we were able to see a pair of buzzards through our binoculars, effortlessly soaring on the air currents above. Swinging my bins along the hill below us I spotted two roe deer: completely oblivious to us they were quietly grazing, watching two walkers on the road below.

'Dae ye think that perr ur walkers then?' I asked Rab.

'Whit, the deer?' said Rab.

'Naw, yon perr oan the road.'

'Aye probably – merr likely thir Munro baggers stretchin thir legs afore headin fur the big hills.'

The tiny figures strode purposefully along. Only a few short years ago that would have been us sweating up the Humphreys Road with heavy packs full of stones, getting ourselves fit for big things. Now, here we were, a pair of birdwatchers, just pottering about on these wee hills passing a Sunday afternoon. Instead of rocks in the rucksacks Rab would more likely have his filled with cow pats for his garden. It might have been spring but to me it seemed that it was more like our autumn. We knew that we were still able for the big days – well, at least I did – but it was just the two of us now. As our gaze drifted over towards the Gleniffer Braes above Paisley we both exclaimed at the same time, 'Ah wonder where the boays ur noo?' Aye, where indeed? A few long gone, some caught up by time and poor health, others just moved away or drifted off to other things. It was Rab and I in the beginning, and now here we were the last of the lot and after over thirty years still out on hills. But only just: we both knew that at seventy-seven Rab himself was nearing the end of his days on the hills. Time was indeed catching up with us all. As the walkers below disappeared from view I began to wonder what made us head for the hills in the first place. To answer that question we would have to look to the early days that shaped our lives. Drowsy now with the warm sun and the song of the skylarks above I peered farther up the river towards the distant cranes of the last remaining shipyard at Govan – could I hear the distant ringing of steel on steel? – Govan, where it all began for me just over half a century ago.

The Early Years

SEE ME, I'M A GOVANITE born to the song of the Clyde and that song was the boisterous and never-ending cacophony of the rivetters' hammers in the nearby shipyards of Fairfields, Harland and Wolff, and Stephens. Since the time when Govan was a mere village on the banks of the Clyde – but still important enough to be marked on Blaeu's early world maps – my ancestors have lived as simple farmers, salmon fishers and weavers, and then worked in the many shipyard trades that made the Clyde famous. In my own childhood there, south of the Rio Clyde, our daily life revolved around the chorus of distinctive factory horns and whistles and the steady tramp tramp of marching boots early each morning: hundreds of men and women on their way to begin their working day in the shipyards, foundries and engineering works in their uniforms of bunnets and boiler suits.

It was in a humble room and kitchen, with the added luxury of an inside toilet, two-up in a grey tenement in 'Wee' Greenfield Street, that I grew up with my parents and younger brother James. Noisy, bustling Govan was a vigorous place to spend your early years. All along the banks of the Clyde basking in the clamour of the post-war shipbuilding boom there was plenty of work for all. Amid a landscape of grey stone canyons was a flourishing community not unlike that of present-day Partick in the west of Glasgow. There was a multitude of shops of all description on almost every corner in these pre-supermarket days. Within a few minutes' walk we had a choice of about five cinemas, monuments to the Art Deco of the nineteen-thirties. Among the urban sprawl were countless sawdust and spit public houses for the legions of thirsty workers – many a worker arrived home reeking of stale beer, in a foul mood, having spent most of their wages. Many a long-suffering wife would resort to the pawn-shops seemingly on every other corner, where meagre family valuables were pawned for money to clothe and feed hungry souls.

Dirt and smells permeated everything. Unlike today's world of showers and bathrooms, smells were an inescapable fact of life. Few people washed regularly, as not everyone had the luxury of a bath in their home. It did not matter if you did bathe often, you only had to sit next to work-ers who wore the same dirty clothes travelling to and from work on the old trams, the steam trains, the subway. As children we bathed in the tin bath in front of the fire. When not in use the bath was kept under the box bed: contrary to popular belief the coal was kept not in the bath but in a bunker either in the lobby (hallway) or on the stairheid (landing). When I left school aged fifteen to work in the foundry you had a bath at the local public baths on a Friday after work. I can still remem-ber the smell of yellow pine the very first day I started my time in the patternshop. It was the one and only time you ever smelled the wood. The

Peter with mother,
brother James and a friend

foundry itself had a distinctive smell not unlike the old Glasgow subway or, in later years, the smell that greeted you as you approached the aluminium town of Kinlochleven.

Outside toilets, no bathrooms, coal fires. I don't suppose any-one would care to live in the conditions we did then. But if you had experienced living with your front door never locked, you would miss the closeness of tenement living. Bureaucratic vandals masquerading as city planners needlessly tore down many a fine sandstone tenement which could easily have been stone-cleaned and refurbished. Sometimes I wonder if this was belated revenge by the Glasgow Corporation on the people of Govan who in 1912 were absorbed into Glasgow. Many Govanites have long maintained that Glasgow should have been swallowed up by Govan. How would it have been, living in the city of Greater Govan? Whole streets disappeared or were re-aligned. New housing replaced the tenement where I lived, and many Govanites were scattered to the sprawling soulless deserts of Drumchapel, Pollok or Castlemilk. But when I grew up, in the fifties and sixties, Glasgow and Clydeside were very different places.

As a small boy on my own I was a terrible wanderer, often crossing back and forth on the wee double-ended passenger ferries or the larger car ferries at Water Row or Meadowside or Linthouse to explore distant places such as Partick and Whiteinch, never dreaming that when I later went to work in Clydebank I would spend many a cold, dark, misty morning crossing the river on these small craft. Now and then two of them would pass in mid-river, eery and silent, packed stem to stern with workers. It was ironic that years later I helped to convert one of these ferries into a restaurant barge that now plies the waters of the restored Forth and Clyde Canal.

For our annual family holidays we nearly always went 'doon the watter' at the 'Glesga Ferr', sailing all the way from the Broomielaw to Dunoon, Cumbrae or Rothesay and occasionally to more remote places like Carrick Castle and Ardentinny on Loch Goil to escape the grime of the city. I was captivated by Scotland's scenery, especially the solitude of Loch Goil where Carrick Castle has sat squarely on the rocky shore since the fifteenth century or even earlier. My brother and I explored it. Although roofless and with no interior floors the walls are intact. There was no access to the battlements, but one of the adults found a ladder and from the first floor we climbed up onto the battlements. The views could not be beaten by any other castle in Cowal.

It was at Carrick that my brother nearly drowned. The old chap whose flat we stayed at had taken us across the loch in a leaky old rowing boat that, when I think about it, was dangerously over-crowded. There were two or three women including my mother and a bunch of us kids. The old guy Wullie rowed right across to the other desolate side for a picnic. On the way we saw a submarine surfacing and diving so it must have been very deep. It was when we returned and were all getting out of the boat that James fell into the water – it was only thanks to a bit of quick thinking by one of the adults that he was pulled out onto the jetty, gasping for air. I can still see him there, under the surface of the crystal-clear waters.

To a wee townie like me there was something magical about exploring the countryside in those days. Maybe it was because there was so little traffic on the roads – most of them were mere single tracks with passing places. What transport there was – from the bustling little steamers with their red and black funnels, to the little cream, red and green buses with the highlander painted on the back that served the Highlands and were a sharp contrast to the drab tram-cars of the city – seemed to belong to a certain David MacBrayne, for whom it was said: 'The Earth is the Lord's, and all it contains, except the Western Isles, which belong to MacBrayne's.'

To look at I must be the most unlikely climber and walker that you could possibly imagine, a diminutive five-foot-nothing in stocking soles, living proof of everything bad about tenement life. All that was missing was the TB and rickets. I don't consciously remember when and where the idea of climbing came from, but we grew up with a playground that consisted of old wash-houses, middens and air-raid shelters left over from the war. 'Dreepin aff dykes' was a hard game that honed our climbing skills: falls often resulted in broken limbs or, worse, a belt around the ears from your parents. Life in the back courts had its own pecking order where you also had to learn to stand up for yourself. This meant bare-knuckle fights. I suppose I was lucky; I only had to experience this at first hand on two occasions. The first time I fought another lad toe to toe and I won, battering his face to a bloody pulp. However the next time my opponent was a lot bigger than me and I was the one who received a bloody nose. Because of my size, at school no one ever selected me for team games such as football. This never really bothered me at all. Despite this I enjoyed physical education in school: the little guys like me were usually placed at the front of the PE class and were always expected to do more. I was probably an ideal shape and stature for climbing, yet when I was little I was always being sent away to residential schools or homes to be built up. I was so skinny, undersized and undernourished that I could get both legs down one trouser leg. Every summer I would be taken along to our family doctor to be weighed and have my height checked: I can still remember my mother filling my trouser pockets with nuts and bolts to make me appear heavier.

I must have been a very average pupil at school. There were subjects that I excelled at and others I struggled with. It was only when I was well through my education that it was realised that I had very short eyesight. I eventually wore glasses constantly but this was after many horrible and nauseating sessions of having drops put in my eyes, making my vision terribly blurred for up to two days at a time. I'm sure that my poor eyesight greatly hindered my school work. I was also left-handed: this is not much of a problem today but when I was at school I was often given the tawse and chastised continuously in an effort to make me write with my right hand.

I gladly left school at fifteen, fortunately at a time when jobs were fairly plentiful, and went to serve my time as a patternmaker in the huge iron foundry known as the 'glass house' of Harland and Wolff in Govan. The foundry was a hard, dirty and dangerous place to work in. My old man suffered his first heart attacks while there. I often used to smile years later when people would say that hard work never killed anyone. I wonder how long they would have lasted in the 'glass house'? I had the knack of reading and producing engineering drawings and I soon found myself working in the relatively clean patternshop instead of in the great dirty foundry. This seemed to cause some resentment with the many apprentice moulders who worked in the foundry: they thought that we had a soft, clean and easy time in the patternshop. On more than a few occasions I was beaten up and left lying with broken spectacles and a bloody nose in the works canteen with the patternmakers' tea-cans scattered on the floor around me – even my front teeth were knocked out after one such going over. In such a place you learned to fight, tell jokes or run like hell. I learned the last two.

When Harland and Wolff closed down their shipbuilding, engineering and foundry works on the Clyde I found myself at eighteen serving the last few years of my apprenticeship in John Brown's patternshop in Clydebank. It was here I met and struck up a lifelong acquaintance with my good friend and comrade Rab Doyle. Rab was the tradesman and I was the apprentice, at work and on the hills. When I first met Rab he was in his early forties. At that time, I now suppose, he was going through what today would be described as a mid-life crisis. He had begun to rebel against the system that swung between a hunger and a burst – employment and the dole – and had taken a long hard look at his priorities. He had just gone through a rather messy divorce after a bitter marriage. He decided to escape the suffocating chains of working for a living as a patternmaker in the shipbuilding industry and set off to wander about Scotland's hills for the next thirty-odd years, occasionally dabbling in the old work ethic with spells at the window-cleaning and with me, repairing a few boats.

Another good friend and early climbing partner at that time was John (Tyrone) Cuthill, an apprentice like myself. John came from the town of Dumbarton, which he liked to point out was the ancient capital of Strathclyde. The three of us formed an alliance and spent many of these early days on the hills together. When John was eventually paid off he spent a few years drifting around till we all lost touch, and eventually he married and settled down in Bournemouth on the south coast of England, sadly about as far from the mountains as you can get.

I went to work in Clydebank in early 1968 simply because, coming from a family with a long history of shipbuilding tradition, I wanted to be involved in building the new Cunard liner which eventually became the QE2 (but to us who worked on her she was always the 'Great Q4'). When the ship was finished, ship-building's fortunes on the Clyde seemed to suddenly decline. There were always large-scale redundancies whenever a ship was finished, but the completion of the QE2 left many with a feeling that the great days of building large ships were over. In Brown's, to encourage men to leave 'voluntarily', the company offered a fifty pounds tax-free severance handshake. Rab Doyle must have seen the writing on the wall and was right there pushing his way to the front of the queue. With his fifty quid bonus on top of his wages he shouldered his tool box and set off along the canal bank. Halfway to his home in Linnvale he thought, 'Fuck this for a gemme o sodjers.' Setting down the heavy box full of the tools of his trade he took out what he thought might possibly be of use. The rest he heaved as far as he could into the middle of the Forth and Clyde Canal. With a satisfying splash and trail of bubbles his chains of slavery sank from sight. Never again would Rab Doyle work at the oppressive petty trade of patternmaking. He never did! Although when the canal was being filled in to make it shallower he lived in a state of panic for weeks in case his box of tools was recovered – it was the tradition for tradesmen to stamp their names on tools such as chisels and so on. He could only breathe freely again when the canal was finally filled in.

Over the years Rab and I used to discuss what inspired us to go to the hills, and what made us seem like loners and eccentrics to our peers who followed the herd – those contemporaries who spent their leisure time caught up in the mindless tribalism of football and sectarianism which is endemic to the West of Scotland. So what did it matter if you were a Proddy or a Tim? – the hills were the great levellers. We were sure that it was a lot to do with the emotional and mental baggage we all carried from our parents and childhood backgrounds. We have a saying in Glasgow that someone mad, bad or just plain daft 'must huv bin drapped oan his heid when he wis a wean'. I suppose it must have applied to most of us. When I was about eighteen months old I was sitting in a rocking horse beside an open coal fire as my mother dozed in a chair. As it rocked nearer and nearer to the fire it struck the hearth, catapulting me headfirst onto the burning embers. I was burned around the head, right hand and arm, leaving me with permanent physical scars. This lapse on my mother's part was a constant cause of bad feeling between my parents as I grew up.

My old granny Kemp used to own a small fruit shop on Govan Road near the Govan dry docks. I can remember staying when I was little at her house in Broomloan Road. The building must have been one of the finest mansion-type houses in all of the Govan area. It was said that in the old granny's day, especially during the war, it was one of the biggest brothels on Clydeside.

My old man, like his father and grandfather before him, had served in the Highland Light Infantry – or as he called them, 'Hell's Little Infidels' – from 1936 till 1946, and had fought through the whole of the desert campaigns in North Africa, Eritrea, Syria, France, Germany and Palestine. He had seen and done things that had left him deeply disturbed with terrible mood swings. I once saw a photograph of two guys in German Afrika Corps uniform on a motorcycle in a desert sandstorm. When I told him that one of the men looked uncannily like him he just shrugged and said that from time to time things got rather chaotic. Although normally a hardworking and generous man, it was strong drink that brought his dark side to the fore. As a boy the time of the year I feared most was Christmas and New Year. We had plenty of gifts and such, but at New Year with the demon drink father turned into a raging monster. Through drink the house would be wrecked and mother beaten, and I frequently felt his metal-studded leather belt across my bare legs. Sometimes for the most trivial misdemeanour I would be belted and thrown out of the house into the close clad only in my underwear, no matter whether it was summer or winter. To make things worse the hidings made me wet my bed for a long time. I was even sent to a clinic that I realised in later years was for seriously disturbed children.

One particular incident that has plagued me for many years occurred on Hogmanay night when I was nine years old. Long after the 'bells' and after a vicious New Year row, my mother, with my brother and me, sought refuge at her sister's house after the old man had gone on a drunken orgy, smashing the house up. In the early hours he smashed the door down and broke in bran-

Father with Granny Kemp
at Broomloan Road

dishing an axe. He forced us to dress and made to walk us home through a deserted Govan. As he herded us along Govan Road, raining punches at us, my mother whispered to me to run for help, fearing that he was going to kill us all. Something snapped in me, fear and terror I don't know, because in a flash I was off and running as fast as I could from near the Govan cross, up past the looming walls of the Harland and Wolff ship-yard, by the old Plaza cinema – almost the whole length of an empty, rain-swept Govan Road – pursued by my axe-wielding father. As I ran along with my heavy shoes echoing on the cobblestones and splashing through puddles I could hear someone screaming – I did not realise till later that it was me. As I burst into the old Govan police station in Orkney Street, the old man gave up the chase and melted into the night. I only stopped the hysterics when slapped across the face by a big burly heilan polis sergeant. Mother never pressed charges, but for me the trauma of that night lasted a long time. For years afterwards I used to wake up at night screaming and when I was married I would scare the life out of my wife, May. So it was probably little wonder that, like so many of my generation, we had these personal demons that shaped our lives. I suppose if such abuse happened today I would have ended up in the care of some social work department. Being a Govanite in those days you just got a slap around the ear and were told to get on with your life. People who knew me always said that I had a chip on my shoulder. Personally I thought that I was quite a level-headed wee bastard with a chip on each shoulder.

Rab Doyle carried his own personal baggage from his childhood days. Many a time as we walked the lang Scots miles at the end of a long gruelling day on the hills he would tell me his life story. If I've heard it once I've heard it a hundred times. Although Rab was born and bred in Clydebank his folks came from Glasgow's East End from a long line of textile workers. One of his earliest memories was of sitting looking out of his window beside Brown's yard watching one of the old Empress liners being launched. When he was only a young lad his mother ran away from home, leaving him and his brothers and sister to be brought up by his old granny and an uncaring father. The one tale he always told was about when, after school, he had to take his faither's greyhounds for exercise no matter the time of year and whatever the weather. The dogs were kept in a small yard beside the canal. He recalls one miserable wet winter's night arriving home after walking them, hungry, no coat, and soaked to the skin. As he stood dripping in the kitchen his old man, hunched over the coal fire, glanced up from his newspaper with a cursory stare and grunted 'Huv yi fed an dried the dugs yet?' Rab always as long as I've known him has relished eating brown bread – not for healthy eating but because the hated greyhounds were always fed on brown bread and meat while Rab and his brothers lived on leftover scraps.

In the thirty-odd years I have known Rab Doyle he has been described by others who knew him as a philanderer, a waster, or a womaniser. I would have to agree to all three and add that he was probably a silly old fool as well. Rab always chased after the women, unable to hold down any long-term relationship. I don't think he could handle real responsibility: his passion for women was just wanting to be mothered. However, for most of the time it never interfered with going to the hills. For a while he had a particular lady 'friend' who used to bake excellent shortbread for services rendered. For months at a time he would come away with the boys with increasing amounts of this home-made shortbread. Large biscuit tins would be handed round at the start of many walks. Eventually, to our relief, he stopped seeing her – by this time we were getting thoroughly sick of the sight of shortbread despite its excellent quality. It would have been nice if he had got a girlfriend who could make cloutie dumpling. At one time he appeared at a Fringe show in Edinburgh as Robert Burns, a role that he seemed to fit perfectly in life.

As the years rolled on and our friends faded from the hills, Rab often speculated that to die in the hills would be no such a bad thing. A few years ago a body was found on a remote mountain-side dressed in cowboy clothing with an empty whisky bottle and a revolver by its side. This impressed Rab greatly and he raved on about it for ages. He always said that if anything ever happened to him on the hills I was not to get too upset but just cover him up and leave him. At one time I probably would have done so since at the time he had no decent gear worth having. However, he recently spent a lot of money on an expensive set of water-proof clothing and if he had dropped dead on the hills then, true to the club code, he would have been stripped of his belongings and left lying in the buff.

In recent years, when we had the opportunity to spend longer in the hills, we often came home earlier than planned. Sometimes we would agree that we had done what we had come to do. Often we agreed to cut trips short if the weather was bad. But more often than not he was suffering from the effects of drink, or increasingly he just wanted home to go up to Glasgow chasing skirt. Eventually he changed his mind about dying on the hills, preferring to expire in some girlfriend's bed. According to Rab himself he 'died' many a time in many a 'burd'z' bed.

Our first outings in the big outdoors were in fact not to the hills but to Loch Lomond, to shoot wild duck and geese. When I say wild, they were in fact almost tame; we sometimes lured them out of places like Luss Bay onto the open loch and then blasted them to pieces. I can still recall shivering uncontrollably in the bow of the boat, standing armed with an oar, smashing the ice as we crept out of Balmaha Bay on a dark freezing morning to endure the bitter cold of another long winter day on the loch. The shooting was just a passing phase. It was something I was never happy with, killing wildlife for sport. I suppose many people go through such phases, especially in their youth, but it is a sad person who does not grow out of them. There were a few lighter moments, though. One time, as we were cruising near the narrows on a particularly misty morning, Rab spotted several ducks sitting in a little bay. I was in the bows with the binoculars and trying to spot what they were, but before I could say anything I was deafened by Rab blasting away above me with a pump-action shotgun. As the gun smoke cleared, a figure emerged from nearby rushes shouting and bawling and waving his arms in a most unfriendly way. Rab in his haste had blasted another hunter's decoys.

On fine winter days on the loch you had to be blind not to notice the magnificence of snow-clad Ben Lomond as a backdrop, and the surrounding Arrochar hills. It was on these Arrochar Alps, on such classic hills as the Cobbler, Ben Ime and Ben Narnain, that we spent many of our early days: a rich learning experience. From their craggy tops, on the few good days, we glimpsed sight of other mountains filling the horizon, which only fired our imagination. We learned the hard way to read maps and navigate on our own as there were few guidebooks to show the way. We knew and cared nothing of Munro's Tables and little or nothing of mountaineering history or the likes of the SMC and other such walking and climbing clubs.

Our sole inspiration for going to the mountains came from the great unemployed masses from Clydeside who pioneered the outdoor revolution in the period between the two World Wars. On our early outings we were encouraged and inspired by one Dan McPhee. Dan was an amiable old patternmaker who had taken Rab on early trips to the hills before the war. His background was West Highland and he used to joke that he had a paraffin tele-

Peter takes aim on Loch Lomond

vision: in fact he must have been one of the last people in Glasgow to use gas lighting in his house. He came from Kelvinhaugh – his war cry was, 'Ah come frae the Haugh an ah fear fuck all.' Dan would describe patternmakers as 'widden engineers'. In Brown's he took us under his wing. Whenever we were planning an outing

Dan would dig out his wee ancient Gall and Inglis guidebooks to Scotland and talk us through our routes. He used to say to us, 'If ye wannt tae find yerselves, awa oot an get loast!' We were very much in awe of the uncanny way he always seemed to know so much about the various places we went to. Over the coming years we eventually did far more on the hills than he ever did and discovered that often he would simply be using a mixture of common sense and bluff. I would like to think that he would have been well pleased that he had in his own way sent us off on the right path. Our heroes were the hardy Clydesiders who went to the hills in the hungry thirties when there was no work. In the seventies and eighties, by courtesy of a certain Mrs Thatcher, we often found ourselves in the same situation.

We never, ever gave a thought to fitness. How could we? There were no fancy gyms then. Working in the jobs we did, we were definitely more likely to be unfit – working with dangerous chemicals, lifting awkward and heavy loads. The only thing that gets you fit for the hills is more hills. In those early days we were pretty timid and at the first sign of bad weather we scampered off the hill as fast as possible; part of the learning process, I suppose. Our equipment was very basic. Gore-tex had not yet been invented. We wore or adapted whatever we could lay our hands on: heavy working waterproof jackets or leggings which left you soaked in your own condensation, even leggings that resembled cowboy's 'chaps'. Sou'westers and huge yellow cycle capes were part of our hill wear too. Footwear was the same boots you wore to your work. Real leather climbing boots for the likes of us were just too expensive. Also, good boots were heavy and cumbersome, crippling to wear, leaving you with painful ankles. I can still remember John Cuthill at the bar wearing his outrageously huge heavy boots, steaming (drunk) but able to lean over at ridiculous angles without falling on his face.

Rab continually experimented with many types of footwear for

Catch of the day – a greylag goose

the hills. When a cheap pair of Spanish fell boots or Japanese walking boots were deemed useless they often helped to light a bothy fire, sometimes creating poisonous fumes. Other clothing such as trousers were often ex-army, or heavy cords – heavy wet cord breeches would cause painful 'nappy rash' on groin and bum, making us look like bandy-legged wee bachles. Rab for a while wore a dinky pair of Black Watch tartan trews on the hills, topped off with a large black cowboy hat. We had no fancy gaiters. In deep snow we wore our PVC leggings over heavy wool socks: often the snow would get under and before long our feet were wet too. It never occurred to us to carry spare dry clothes. After all, we had to carry everything and we had no car in which to leave a dry change of clothes. At the end of many an outing we travelled home on the bus in our damp clothes, and we wondered why we were sore and stiff for days afterwards.

Sometimes we made use of walking sticks – especially John Cuthill – but not often. Later we acquired ice-axes of indeterminate antiquity. My ice-axe was a gift from an old climber I knew, Swiss-made with a wooden shaft and about three feet long. Rab got his in an Oxfam shop for fifty pence; his was nearer five feet long, just like an old-style alpenstock. He cut a few feet off the thing, but they were always a burden to carry and a constant source of danger to the user and more so to anyone nearby. What we hauled around the hills in our old Bergens to cook with, I still find it hard to believe, especially the metalwork we carried. On more than one occasion we humped three pots, a frying pan, a kettle and a smelly old paraffin stove. We must have been some sight clanking along the byways.

One of the earliest outings to the hills was a trip on the old Midland Bluebird Glasgow-to-Oban bus from the Clydebank Town Hall. We got off the bus at Arrochar and walked around the top of the loch and along the shore road to the youth hostel at Ardgartan. Here we left the main road and continued along the lochside. Our route took us through and over the Coilessan Glen to Lochgoilhead.

The weather was wet and misty and the rain was becoming

heavier as the day wore on. Reaching the village at Lochgoilhead very late in the afternoon we struck the long winding road leading back to the top of the 'Rest and be thankful'. It was totally devoid of any traffic that we could try for a lift as we trudged wearily along. As the daylight began to fade the rain increased to a steady downpour. Instead of waiting for the Glasgow bus at the top of the 'Rest' we walked down onto the old Glen Croe road, now in darkness. When it rejoined the new road we kept peering back, watching for the bus coming down to Glasgow. Now in driving rain and by this time very tired and soaked through, we could suddenly see it approaching. Instantly Rab was out into the middle of the road trying to flag down the coach, waving a wet newspaper.

John Cutill on Ben Vorlich
with his famous heavy boots

Going too fast or not seeing us at all, the driver flew past in a cloud of spray. Sick, we could only struggle wearily on to Arrochar village and hope to catch the later bus coming down from Fort William. On reaching the village we found that the tea room was still open, so in we went for a fry-up of sausages, bacon and eggs. As we dried off in the warm cafe we ended our meal with buttered scones. I was having difficulty finishing but Rab insisted I eat the last morsel. 'Ye cannae leave that. Efter a', ah've pyed fur it,' says he. With Rab growing up in a household where the dugs were better fed than the children, it was unknown ever since for Rab to leave an empty plate – anybody's empty plate – after a meal. It was not unusual for him to ask for the plates to be passed along so that he could mop up the leftovers.

The coaches at that time still had conductresses who, like their Glasgow counterparts, continually policed the length of the bus. As we wound our way down the twisting lochside road I began to feel very queasy, turning a whiter shade of pale, and then green. Finally the motion at the rear of the coach became too much for my delicate stomach. 'Ah'm gonnae be sick,' groans I. At that Rab dived into his bag and produced a plastic bag for me to puke into. 'Here, use this.' Unfortunately all he had was a Marks and Spencer bag which of course has holes all along its bottom. The foul-smelling content quickly ended up on the floor, and as we travelled the undulating switchback road down Loch Long this evil tide of vomit began to wash up and down, stinking the whole coach out. Finally, one by one, the rest of the passengers all joined together in a mass spew-in – even the wee conductress herself succumbed and began to throw up her guts in the aisle and out the front door.

The first Munro I ever climbed was Ben a'Cleibh from Dalmally, with Rab. Our original planning was for a hike of a couple of days to do four Munros. In actual fact we walked in one day from Dalmally to Ardlui via Ben a'Cleibh and avoided climbing Ben Lui because it was too misty. Very soon, however, we were regularly using the Oban bus and tentatively exploring around the Arrochar mountains. We often used my old family caravan based at Ardlui. We would catch the bus at Clydebank Town Hall early on many a winter's morning on a run that was long and tedious. John Cuthill would often join it at the cemetery gates in Dumbarton. We would have a stop for tea at the old Green Kettle Tea Rooms between Garelochhead and Loch Long. In midwinter this was a cold, dank, miserable place. On the journey home – this is supposing we caught the bus – I was nearly always horribly travel sick, a condition that plagued me for years. Quite a few times when we did get lifts, much to Rab's disgust I was soon throwing up and getting us dropped well short of home. On one particular occasion we had got a good lift on a miserable wet day in the back of a small van. In the confined space I soon began to feel ill. Rab went to get a 'sick-bag' out, but too late. 'That's as far as we go lads,' the driver said as he dropped us on the outskirts of Balloch in the rain – a scenario that was repeated many times.

Peter on Ben Oss, with goggles but no gaiters

After I left Brown's and went to work at McGruer's in Clynder in 1973, we often used an old red Ford Transit to go further afield. John Cuthill also had an old A40 saloon car nicknamed the 'Grey Rabbit'. The vehicle had, I'm sure, the wrong size of tyre – when we went round corners they scraped along the bodywork. Often we could never be sure if the thing would start after a long day on the hills. When we could we would try to park on or near a hill and push-start it. There was also the old-fashioned means of turning the engine, by using the dreaded 'starting handle'. Get it wrong and you could break a wrist. One day we parked in a lay-by near Arrochar and came back that night to find the car hemmed in by trailers containing logs. We had no choice but to leave it there, get the service bus home that night and come back up on the bus the next day to retrieve the Rabbit. John Tyrone Cuthill was a wee bit younger than I and had only started his apprenticeship a short time before we were all eventually paid off from Brown's. John and I had many trips to the hills, sometimes together with Rab, other times just the two of us. In those early years, at holidays we took ourselves off into the Highlands for long-distance walks, but more often than not we spent time on hills near home such as the Arrochar and Loch Lomond hills. It was not unusual to find me sitting outside the chapel at Arrochar while Cuthill nipped in for a quick Mass – nursing a hangover – before setting off to climb the Cobbler. During the coming years Cuthill drifted away and we lost touch. Rab and I, however, kept on going and soon began to take the hills by storm. We went on to more and more big outings on the hills. We hammered the Munros. We did big walks: from Fort Augustus to Aviemore by the Corrieyarrick, Speyside, Dalwhinnie Glen Tromie, Glen Feshie, Linn of Dee, the Larig Ghru to Coylumbridge and Aviemore; and many others, culminating in finishing the Munros.

On many hard mountain days, in weather fair or foul, we kept each other's spirits up and in all the years we only came close to blows once. This took place on a mountain which could have been any one of dozens. In thick mist and heavy rain, exhausted and literally soaked to the skin, Rab kept quizzing me about our navigation, which was difficult for me trying to read a wet map through steamed-up glasses. I eventually cracked up.

'Who's daein the fuckin navigatin, me or you?'

'Ah, but!' Rab retorted, 'Aw ma years o experience must coont fur sumthing.'

'Aye, but ah'm the wan wae ra compass!'

By this time we had both grabbed each other by our rucksack straps, unable to swing blows, restricted by the wet waterproofs. Like a pair of mad waltzers we danced about in the mist till, exhausted and shaking with laughter, we collapsed on our backsides in the rain-soaked heather.

By 1989 when we finished the Munros we had climbed and walked over large parts of this wee country of ours. On the way we had made many friends in outdoor clubs such as the Holiday Fellowship and the Glennifer and wherever we tramped. In the end we still went to the hills to climb the Corbetts. We couldn't care less if we finished them. We would always be wee men on big hills.

McAlpine's Fusiliers

THIS MAD VENTURE WAS ONE that should and could so easily have ended in complete disaster. Instead it was just a dismal failure topped off with a massive pub crawl – an ill-planned adventure that highlighted just how innocent, raw and incompetent we were at that time. When people would comment in later years on how experienced we were, I thought with a shudder of yon day on the Ben and could only reply, 'Naw, we wir jist lucky.'

It was the worst time of the year for such rookie climbers as we were. It began one weekend at the end of November. We had hired a Bedford van with the intention of climbing Ben Nevis, in the county of Lochaber in the West Highlands. At 1,340 metres it is the highest mountain in the country. Its very name comes from the Gaelic Beinn-neanh-bhathais: neamh means the heaven or clouds, bhathais, the top of a man's head (between crown and brow). So, 'the mountain with its head in the clouds'. So it was we set off with our heads in the clouds, inspired by our mentor, old Dan McPhee, armed with our large Lion Rampant flag and a shield depicting a lion and the legend 'The Patternmakers' Munro Expedition to Ben Nevis'. On this trip were myself, Rab Doyle, John Cuthill and – for his one and only trip to the hills – my younger brother James. This was the first time I had ever driven beyond Crianlarich at night. In fact it was the first time I had driven anywhere outside the city at night. With the narrowness of the old twisting road up Loch Lomondside, and blinded at times by the headlights of oncoming traffic, I found this a terrifying experience.

As we cleared the top end of the loch we began to make good progress to Crianlarich where we stopped for a pint in the hotel. A wee while later we were again on our way, and soon passed the lights of Bridge of Orchy. The hotel here later became a popular watering hole but in yon days it was an old ex-army type who ran the place. He was well known for his grumpiness. The hotel sold fuel – as it does today – but woe betide you if it was not a substantial enough amount to make it worth the 'Colonel' leaving the bar. As we drove up over the Rannoch Moor we found that we now had the road more or less to ourselves. In the rear, Jim and John had to sit on our gear as there were only the two front seats. This they were quite happy to do as they had a few cans of beer to compensate. As you approach the Kingshouse there is what we call the coat-hanger bridge: there, standing in the middle of it in the full glare of our headlights, was a large red deer stag. This was the first time most of us had seen any red deer at

The Ben Nevis expedition:
James, Rab and Cuthill

such close range. From the back I heard the guys exclaim, 'Wid ye look at the size o yon big beast!' Someone else piped up, 'Aye, look at the size o yon haunle baurs. Ye could hing oot a washin oan them!' Unable to pass, I slowed to a complete halt. Totally unruffled by the glare of the headlights or me tooting the horn at him he turned nonchalantly to face us. Looking up from his grazing with a baleful look about him, he pawed the tarmac and it seemed as though he was about to charge towards us. As he stood there, his breath hanging in the cold air, I slipped into reverse and slowly moved back. Finally, with an indifferent shrug of his antlers, he swaggered off into the night. Truly the Monarch of the Glen, and King of the Road.

We drove on a bit more warily looking out for the many deer we could see grazing at the road's edge, their eyes reflected in the headlights, until we came at last to Glencoe. It was strange to know that we were driving through this famous place surrounded on all sides by mountains we had read about but had never ever seen. We stopped to relieve ourselves at the meeting of the waters which we could not see but could clearly hear pouring off the hills. At this time there was no bridge at Ballachulish to speed on over. Instead we turned to drive the long eighteen miles around Loch Leven. Nine winding miles beyond Glencoe village I was amazed to see the lights of Kinlochleven. I thought at first the hills were on fire. It was so unexpected to see a real town with street lights in what seemed to me was the middle of nowhere. Kinlochleven was one of the first towns in Britain to have electric lighting. We passed on through the deserted main street to a lay-by just beyond the town and settled down for a night on the van floor wrapped in our sleeping bags. Next morning we awoke stiff and cold – the van's thin metal walls held no heat. So after a quick breakfast we drove on.

Fort William had no pedestrian precincts then, just a busy main road. The railway station opposite the pier effectively cut off the town from the loch-side. We turned into Glen Nevis and parked the van just beyond the youth hostel. The Ben Nevis path starts opposite the hostel by crossing the bridge here over the River Nevis. The old pony track itself actually begins much farther down the glen at Auchintee Farm. The hostel track joins this older track and then contours around the hillside past Windy Corner and into where the Red Burn lies. It was dull, wet and misty as we set off. I had a balaclava knitted by my ma. James in his black beret looked uncannily like Che Guevara. Cuthill had an authentic-looking woollen balaclava while Rab had a black sou'wester. So, looking like a right bunch of mountain men, off we went. It was not long before we were sweating and soaked through with rain and condensation. Our cheap waterproofs, ex-navy foul-weather jackets and thin leggings, were practically useless. James, at this time a pretty fit guy, was soon charging on ahead while the rest of us struggled up the rough track. Cuthill as usual was suffering from condensation and dehydration, or the DTs. Where the path turns into the Red Burn we had a welcome halt for food and a hot drink. It was sheltered at this point from the wind and rain but becoming very grey and overcast. Today at the Red Burn the track now veers away to avoid following the burn because of serious erosion, but then it just followed it on up to join the zigzag path up to the summit plateau.

As we emerged onto the bealach between the Ben and Meal an t-Suidhe we began to feel the full force of a rising gale. It was also starting to snow and the brooding mass of Nevis was lost in a white curtain. Above and to the right of where the old halfway house stood we turned into the teeth of the gale and with great difficulty pushed on to the sheltered corner where the burn re-crosses the pony track. As we gathered here we had a discussion as to what we should do. To continue would be to invite disaster but we were reluctant to give in at this stage. So we looked at our maps and decided that we might try to gain the summit by the route up past the CIC hut and on to the arête by the abseil posts.

With the wind now behind us we soon retraced our steps and were crossing the open ground in deep snow heading for the Alt a'Mhuillin path. Crossing this stretch was made difficult by the now gale-force winds and snow. Our useless skins were thoroughly soaked through with condensation that began to freeze inside them. Without ice-axes we floundered about in the snow. As we dropped into the Alt a'Mhuillin we dropped out of the wind which now screamed and howled above our heads. Walking under the mass of the Ben's cliffs we were sheltered from the wind. The path here is rough enough going even on a good day, twisting up and down as it wends its way to the hut. In deepening snow we made poor progress. Halfway to the hut, exhausted by struggling in the deep snow, we decided to call it off. Visibility was by now reduced to almost white-out conditions, the towering cliffs of the Ben lost in a white void.

By crossing the bealach we had cut off our line of retreat. Besides, we were too wet, miserable and cold to even try to go back the way we came. Our only avenue of escape off the hill was to follow the Alt a'Mhuillin down to wherever it would take us – even if it meant a long walk back to the van. Finally, as the snow thinned, we regained the path for a short time. Once more in the lee of the hillside, rather than walk out to the golf course we turned off the track to contour round the bulk of Meal an t-Suidhe above the aluminium works and eventually into Glen Nevis itself to straggle back to the van.

Onto the bealach

As the weather had now gone to pieces we abandoned the idea of camping in the glen. After changing into dry clothes we drove into the Fort seeking food and drink. Starting at one end we proceeded to have a drink in every public house on Fort William High Street. Up one side and down the other. Most of the bars then were typical barren Highland bars, tacky tartan and formica. After Rab and Cuthill had tried to chat up the barmaid in the old Station Bar, we moved along to the Volunteer Arms where an Irish navvy wanted to have a square-go with James amid a heated debate on the properties of concrete as building material . Having drunk our way round the High Street, we decided for some mad reason to go further north for more drink, and drove up past Spean Bridge to the Invergarry Hotel. Its bar was a small building set apart along the road from the main hotel. In we breezed, singing McAlpine's Fusiliers. A small bar was in the far corner diagonally opposite from the door, in another corner was a fireplace, and in the last there were some ancient tables and chairs. A few local worthies were propping up the bar, their bleary eyes rubbering round the room at our entrance. One a least was propped upright with a large sweeping brush. At their feet lay three sorry-looking sheepdogs that balefully gazed at us for a moment. Sitting at a rickety table were a pair of middle-aged out-of-season tourists. As the night drove on and we all became fu and unco happy, everyone began to join the fun. Even the jaded locals commandeered tin whistles and mouth organs we had with us. Dogs howled at the moon, and Rab fell in love singing to the wee tourist whose husband slowly slid under the table full of the water of life.

When we finally made it back to the van we were all pretty drunk and it was too late to even think about pitching a tent. Being the least drunk, I decided to drive to a lay-by just outside of the Fort, planning for us all to crash out in the back. Easier said than done. Full of spirits and fighting drunk, James wanted to round off the night with a customary bar-room brawl, with me as his sparring partner. As we all wrestled about in the back of the van, cursing, swearing and swinging blows, Rab – well-known pacifist and unused to a bit of friendly violence – jumped out onto the road near to tears shouting, 'Ah've hud enuff o you lot, ahm walking hame ya bunch o' mad bastards!' In the mayhem that ensued, James, unwilling to forego his fun, got hold of one of the shovels we were carrying in case of snow drifts. Swinging this about in the confined space he sliced the headrest off the driver's seat, then almost took a slice out of the side of the vehicle as we dodged his wild swings in the rocking van. While his spade was tangled in some rucksacks I shouted to John to lamp him with the other spade. Missing him, he hit me instead. I saw stars. This I thought was a bit odd, especially as I was by now lying on the floor and looking up at the tin roof. Wincing as I felt the side of my head, I realised that I was nursing a growing lump on my skull. I started yelling, 'Hit him, no me.' We eventually subdued him with a swift and this time accurate blow to the head from another spade. We then poured him, suitably unconscious, into his sleeping bag and trussed him up with our climbing rope – or, to be more accurate, my mother's washing line. To Rab, outside on the road, we shouted, 'Come oan, get back in the van ya stupid auld bugger an stoap yir bloody greetin! It's too bloody faur tae walk hame tae Glesga at this time o night. So get back in the van or we'll brain you wi the shovel an aw, ye daft oul bastart.' Eventually we all struggled into our sleeping bags as best as drunks could and settled down for what remained of the night.

Or so we thought. We hadn't in our drunken state realised just how cold it would be inside a thin metal box as the temperature dropped way below freezing. In the middle of the night I awoke with my teeth chattering uncontrollably, and much to my disgust found that I was soaked through. One of the others had tried to get up for the toilet, pissed all over me, and then passed out. Cursing, I threw a boot at the pile of snoring bastards whose only response was a series of grunts. I thought about giving them a drop of their own medicine but it had been enough trouble getting them all to settle down in the first place. So, wet and freezing, I had no option but to get up and change into some dry clothes.

There was no point in getting back into a wet sleeping bag so I decided to drive south to our old caravan at Ardlui. At least, once moving, I could get the heater going. Starting the van up had no impression on the three others lying in a drunken stupor in the back. At least the night was dry. At this late hour nothing moved and we were rather low on fuel. At Onich there was a petrol station where you could obtain fuel by using a pump that took money. I had to go through the others' pockets to find the right change, taking the opportunity to land a few well-aimed kicks on the buggers blissfully snoring away. Every place we passed was deathly silent as I drove on, back through Ballachulish, Kinlochleven and around the loch to Glencoe. It began to snow ever so slightly. The headlights showed an empty road as they picked out the few landmarks. Beyond the meeting of the waters as we emerged from the glen the snow began to fall thicker and heavier. As the glen opened up by Altnafeidh the snow drove horizontally across my line of vision. As we passed the darkened Kingshouse and crept onto the Moor of Rannoch it became harder to see the road, which was being covered by drifting snow. The van lurched about, difficult to steer, and still the others slept on. Progress was down to a crawl. As we neared Loch Ba I hit a deeper drift and lost control. We slewed across the road till, with a lurch, the rear wheels slammed into the ditch.

On the way home, a sorry bunch

Shaken and well awake I switched the engine off and got out into the driving snow for a look. I climbed into the back to look for a shovel, stamping deliberately on the still-snoring inert bodies. Back in the blizzard with a sack and spade I was trying to dig us out when Rab wakened and came out to help. Between the both of us we rocked the vehicle back and forth till it lurched back on to the road. Frozen, we got going again.

Beyond Bridge of Orchy – no signs of life, its buildings covered in snow just like a Christmas-card scene – the blizzard began to ease off. As we laboured up the long straight towards Tyndrum the first ragged streaks of dawn appeared in a torn sky. When we reached the caravan park at Ardlui, Rab and I opened up my old caravan, lit both the cooker and gas fire and then, digging out all the bedding we could find, crawled into the bunks. The other two we left in the van sound asleep, unaware that we had arrived at Ardlui. When they awoke they remembered nothing of the previous night's antics or the drive.

When we reached Glasgow that night we learned that the same storm that had chased us off the Ben had lashed the Cairngorms. A party of teachers and schoolchildren had perished on the Cairngorm plateau trying to reach shelter in white-out conditions.

Hard Times

AS 1971 BEGAN, UNKNOWN to many of us there were world events stirring that would affect many lives for years to come. Shipbuilding on the Clyde went spiralling into decline, leaving only two shipbuilding yards to stagger on from one ship to another. In March that year I became engaged to my future wife and we were wed the following year. Since then, long-suffering May has stoically put up with my many disappearances to the hills. But as 1973 came to a close I found myself out of work for the first time. The previous October had witnessed a short but bitter clash between Arab and Israeli. Emerging oil-producing nations grasped control of their own oil production and this in turn plunged the Western world into economic crisis. Industrial unrest became the norm throughout Britain as the mining industry realised its new-found strength and coal became king once more. Constant clashes between trade unions and the government of the day soon led to widespread electricity cuts to homes and industry. Fifty-miles-per-hour speed limits were imposed, TV was blacked out after ten-thirty at night, petrol was in short supply, shops were cleared of food through panic-buying, and one million people in Britain were out of work.

It was against the backdrop of these troubled times that my long career in boat building began. Not long after I was made redundant from Brown's in November 1972, desperate for a job, I found myself working for the old family yacht-building firm of McGruer in their yard at Clynder on the shores of the Gareloch. At the start of 1973, while most people were still enjoying their New Year holidays, I was starting my new career as a boat builder with a sharp culture shock. In my previous workplaces I was used to working in a fairly warm and clean environment. Now I travelled miles to work in the back of an old van, and me cursed with my terrible travel sickness. In winter we froze in the dark unheated sheds and in summer we sweltered under a hot tin roof you could fry eggs on. In the six years I spent working on the quiet back-waters of the Gareloch I learned a great deal about the skills required in building boats, from sleek wooden-hulled yachts to high-speed plastic motor-cruisers.

Yet neither these events nor married life stopped me going to the hills. In the early years of our marriage, like most couples, we would clash frequently as May tried to mould me to be like other

Peter at McGruers

domesticated men. 'Unbreakable' plates and crockery as well as knives and forks would be left embedded in doors and walls, and occasionally the dinner ended up in the dog. May eventually came to recognise that my going to the hills was a necessary safety valve for both of us. Women have a way of making their men feel guilty, especially if they think their partner is enjoying something, yet in reality when we are out of sight they are only too glad to be rid of us. In fact I have to admit that I was luckier than most married men. Wee May never really stopped me going to my hills and on the few occasions when she came with me she proved to be an excellent hillwalker. The funny thing was, May never liked exposed ridges or being near steep drops, yet when we lived on the top floor of a three-storey Glasgow tenement she thought nothing of sitting on the narrow window ledge to clean the windows. I was too terrified to do this myself – the window frames were ancient and riddled with rot, and had the unnerving habit of coming away in your hands, leaving you sitting on the window ledge three storeys up holding a complete window frame. I used to make her tie a rope around her waist (or was it her neck?) when window cleaning. Over the years we produced four great boys. Often this seemed to be the result of long trips to the hills.

Corrour to Fersit

WE HAD A SUPERB EASTER trip when we ventured into the midst of the Central Highlands. Driving to Dumbarton Station very early in the morning it was our intention to catch the early morning sleeper to Fort William and to get off at the isolated station at Corrour. Dumbarton was the first station after Glasgow where the Highland train stopped. In the early morning there was often no one on duty in the ticket office to sell us a ticket. So we would nonchalantly board the train when it stopped. Even now the sound of yon old diesel engines thrumming away in the distance still sets the pulse racing. Once aboard, we would quickly settle down and catch some sleep on the long haul along the north shores of the Clyde. We would pass Craigendoran and then, on the steel of the old West Highland Line, begin the long slow climb up by the Gareloch.

When we finally reached the lonely Corrour station, 500 metres above sea level, we stepped off the train on the side away from the platform without being asked for our fare. We were in an area that to us was as remote and desolate as the moon. It was a dry but biting cold morning as we walked the short distance to Loch Ossian and the youth hostel. Although it was early in the season and the hostel was not yet officially open we were confident that we would find shelter there that night, and so we had decided not to carry a tent with us on this outing. It was an area with very little shelter, but we had thought it too cold for camping out so early in the year.

When we arrived at the old hostel it was indeed unlocked and open, and there was certainly someone in residence, judging by the number of sleeping bags and quantity food lying about. But we were sure that two wee Glesga punters could squeeze into some corner, and so off we went to climb our hills – but not before we helped ourselves to a little bit of everything from all the food lockers and had ourselves a fine breakfast. We noted that a new (English) warden had recently been appointed. He had gone home at the end of the season leaving a pair of binoculars hanging in his quarters with a note saying that they had been too heavy to carry, and that he would collect them on his next visit. Well of course they had long gone, but another note had been left in their place saying 'Thanks!'.

Our climb began right away up onto the old Road to the Isles path. It was a bitterly cold day on the tops. As we climbed there was snow, not deep but soft and with plenty of spindrift, and the going was slow. Carn Dearg was the first Munro that day and from its summit we went down and then up onto Sgor Gaibhre. From here we turned north over Sgor Choinnich to face a long rough descent to the east end of Loch Ossian.

When we got back to the hostel there were about twenty or so English chaps there. At first they did not say much and did seem rather stand-offish. Still, we assumed that it was OK for us to stay. This was one of the first encounters we ever had with anyone from England in the Scottish outdoors. Nevertheless they obviously had formed a committee, as Englishmen do, and had held a meeting and duly appointed a spokesman to inform us that they had booked the hostel for their sole use and that we had to leave. On hearing this I was incensed – I was all for throwing the bloody lot of the buggers out. For goodness sake there were only twenty of them and the two of us. It seemed to me that the odds were pretty even. It was no wonder that it took me many years to end my dislike of the English as a nation, despite having made many good English friends over the years.

Angry and disgusted we packed up our gear and went out into the gathering dusk. The sky being crystal-clear meant that it would be a long cold night and we had no place to shelter. We were furious at the idea of being cast out by a bunch of bloody Englishmen. Such a thing would never have happened if it had been the other way around. Everyone would have made space for two wee men. What were we to do? It was too late to catch a train home. There was no shelter or bothy for miles and the temperature was dropping fast. We walked round the north side of the loch and came to a small log cabin, but it was filthy, wide open to the elements, with no windows and no fireplace. There was only one thing we could do – walk back along the loch past the hostel to Corrour Station and see if the station master could offer us some shelter.

The station master, Charlie, was a bit of a character. It was rumoured that he ran a brothel in Dundee but obviously he liked playing with trains. He told us to use the old station waiting room and to help ourselves to a huge pile of coal nearby. The waiting room was the original old West Highland Line building: no furniture, just the bare wooden floor. Now the building is an upmarket bunkhouse with facilities for today's Munro-baggers. The fireplace was a real bonus. With the coal on the platform nearby we found a shovel and soon got to work, and that night as we lay there on the hard wooden floor we were as warm as toast, with the room lit by a roaring fire and the shadows dancing on the walls. We had the last laugh: we knew those miserable petty Englishmen must be huddled in their sleeping bags trying to sleep in a cold hostel devoid of any heat whatsoever.

We woke as the sun streamed in through the window next morning. The fire was out and it was cold to stick your nose out of the comfy sleeping bags. Outside was a winter wonderland. In all directions a white landscape of pristine snow sparkled in the sunlight. All was still. The station was buried in a white coat. Even the railway track was covered. The water taps outside had frozen solid.

Our plan that morning was to make for Loch Treig. As we struggled through the deep snow, nothing else moved; all was white under a clear sky and a blinding sun. Only the occasional trail of animal tracks in the snow gave any sign of life. We followed the railway till the path cuts off down to Loch Treig. At the loch there was less snow and we made our way around the shore. Before starting up our hills we had a drum-up beside the bridge near Creaguaineach Lodge. To the west the path wound its way on through to Glen Nevis. For us, a short walk along the shore and across a small bridge would lead us to the start of the day's climb.

This was a long day traversing the two big Munros of Stob Coire Easan and Stob a Choire Mheadhoin. These hills are quite close together, and this means that there is a steep up-and-down between them. Once over both tops we had a long descent along the northern ridge. At last we stood on the top of Meal Cian Dearg looking down at the top end of Loch Treig. It got colder and the light faded the footprints we had been following in the snow for most of the day, which now dropped down a steepening slope and had become frozen ice. Not equipped with crampons or ice-axes we decided that it would be safer, though a longer route, to retrace our steps back along the ridge and to traverse off the hill at an angle that would bypass the worst part. Almost in darkness we reached the road end at the loch and walked the short distance to Fersit, our destination for the night.

Fersit was probably one of the first independent hostels. It was the home of a Dundee woman, Nancy Smith. Living nearby in an old Leyland Tiger bus was the well-known Dundee hill man Davy Glen. Although Nancy ran the place it was Davy who had built most of it. It was a real hotchpotch of rough wooden buildings with different bits and pieces added on at different times. There were no facilities, no running water or electricity. The bedding was old army blankets that were damp and smelly and never seemed to get washed or aired. Despite all this the place was popular with walkers and climbers from all over.

It was Davy Glen who played a major role in recovering the bodies of the five men who perished in blizzard conditions while attempting to cross Jock's Road from Braemar to Glen Doll on New Year's Day in 1959. When we met him before we set off to walk to Tulloch the next morning for the train home we told him where we had come: he just looked down at us with a baleful grin and shook his head at the pair of us.

Although the railway runs right past Fersit, the nearest station was Tulloch. We walked there along the tracks. When we asked for two tickets to Dumbarton, the station master could not give us change of a ten-pound note – quite a lot of money then – and told us to pay on the train. When the train arrived and we boarded, we saw him talking to the guard and assumed that he was telling him about us. So we changed some of our clothing about and settled down in a corner with our heads down while the guard

Nancy Smith's hostel, Fersit

walked up and down fruitlessly looking for us. When the train pulled into Dumbarton later that night we got off without paying any fare in either direction.

Rannoch to Kinlochleven

IN THE SPRING OF 1973 I undertook a solo cross-country walk from Rannoch Station to Fort William. I had no real plan in mind; I was simply out to wander among the hills. I walked a short distance along the road from the morning train and turned onto the Road to the Isles. This track loosely follows the east side of the West Highland Line to Corrour, in wild remote countryside with little or no habitation. It was a day of sunshine and frequent heavy showers. When they came on I sat down with waterproofs draped over me till they passed. At Loch Ossian youth hostel I found that the warden was related to Rab Doyle. After a night in Ossian I decided to walk to Nancy Smith's hostel at Fersit. A short distance round the shore of Loch Ossian I turned to climb the easy slopes of Beinn na Lap.

The day was dry and warm and the visibility hazy as I progressed up towards the summit cairn with the loch and the hostel just in view. From the cairn I walked a short way along the ridge and then dropped sharply into the deep glen towards the Allt Feith Thuill. On the floor of the glen I became aware of a strange noise. It sounded like someone hitting sticks together and it was getting louder. Suddenly from the right I could see a huge herd of red deer charging towards me through the valley, filling the whole width of the glen and some distance up the hill slopes on each side. Climbing as fast as I could I just managed to get out of their way as they swept past in a heaving mass of hooves and antlers.

Once the deer had passed I climbed steeply up the grassy slopes to the summit of Meal Garbh, which at 977 metres is the south top of Chno Dearg, itself 1,047 metres. Chno Dearg is a rounded, stony but quite featureless hill. From here I retraced my steps for a short way then swung west-north-west down and across to the low bealach to approach Stob Coire Sgriodain by its east ridge, a combination of knobbly tops and two fair drops in height. Once I made the summit of Sgriodain I was rewarded by fine views of

Loch Treig below. My descent was north over the craggy top of Sron na Gharbh Beinne and through forestry at the end of the loch, leaving a short walk to Fersit.

On this visit there was no one at Fersit and I had the place to myself. After a quiet night I was up and away early to catch the train back to Corrour. This short train ride is a spectacular part of the West Highland Line as it runs along the side of Loch Treig.

Graveyard at Kinlochleven dam

Back at Corrour I had a leisurely wander round to the hostel which was quiet. Here I met a wee guy who like myself came from Govan – Tam McGeachy. We both decided to walk through to Kinlochleven the following day.

With an early start next morning we stepped out from Corrour Station on the track running parallel to the railway towards Loch Treig. This would not be the last time I would pass along this way. At the loch, instead of following the trail through into Glen Nevis, we almost immediately turned off into a narrow glen, Gleann Iolairean, and began to climb up by the Allt Feith Chiarain. As the pass narrowed we were soon hemmed in on one side by the crags of Meal a Bhainne and by the bulk of Leum Ulleum on the other. Once over the watershed of the pass we began to descend towards Loch Chiarain. This loch, seemingly in the middle of nowhere, drains into the huge Blackwater reservoir, created in 1904 with the construction of the Blackwater dam – in its time one of the world's largest civil-engineering feats. It was the creation of the reservoir that flooded out the last few inhabitants of the desolate area we were now in. The track was in fact one of the old cattle drovers' routes to the markets in the south.

At the end of Loch Chiarain stands a small building. This was at the time Chiarain bothy and it was in reasonable condition with good accommodation upstairs. It was maintained by the Mountain Bothies Association or MBA. Later I found out that this was a favourite haunt of 'Big Shooie' the reputed 'Paisley poacher'. Shooie was reputed to have had guns hidden nearby to shoot the 'beasties'.

After a good rest at the bothy we set off again on a path leading away towards the reservoir. Near to where the path meets the loch there is a large monument in the shape of a Celtic cross that commemorates a drowning nearby – the details I have long since forgotten. Very soon we came to the dam itself. A close inspection reveals that the structure is not the usual concrete dam but in fact a well-built masonry, early concrete (not smooth like modern concrete but filled with pebbles and stones) and earthen construction. Scouting around at the base of the dam we came across a small graveyard astride a hillock. The headstones were made from the same rough concrete and although a few had names, mainly Irish and Highland, others were marked simply 'Unknown'. There was even the grave of one solitary woman: God only knows what she was doing there among nearly two thousand or so men – maybe she did their laundry. The story of the building of the Blackwater dam is best described by the Irish navvy-turned-writer Patrick McGill, in his book *The Children of the Dead End*.

Leaving the dam we set off the last few miles to Kinlochleven. This part of the path follows the River Leven, now ruined by the dam. It is one of the roughest paths that I have ever encountered in many years of walking. As the sun began to set we staggered into Kinlochleven. The aluminium works were still in operation and you could smell the place before you could see it. It was a smell that reminded me of when I started my trade working in Harland's foundry. We made straight for the local chip shop where we sat outside on the pavement scoffing greasy fish suppers and ginger beer. With full bellies we walked the one-and-a-half miles to Narrach Bridge along the busy A82 – still the main route north prior to the opening of the Ballachulish Bridge in 1975.

After a good night's sleep in my caravan at Narrach Bridge, the next morning we set off up towards the old Mamore Lodge and onto the route of the soon-to-be-opened West Highland Way, where we wearily plodded the last few miles through the Larig Mhor and by Loch Lundavra into Fort William to catch a bus home to Glasgow. Over the next few years I met Tam a few more times as we crossed paths in the Highlands.

Fort Augustus to Aviemore

WHEN I WENT TO WORK FOR McGruer's at Clynder I no longer had my annual holidays at the traditional times such as the Glasgow or Clydebank 'Fair'. We stopped either later or earlier in the year outwith holiday periods so that the yacht owners always had people there to launch, repair and provide services during the sailing season. So this particular year it was well into the month of August when Rab Doyle and I set off on the Fort William bus. In the bus station in Glasgow we met a joiner whom I worked with. It was Jimmy 'Meboza' Ritchie, off to his old home in Burghead. Old Jimmy was a bit of a cyclist in his day. He used to describe how he and a pal would cycle home from Glasgow to Burghead even in winter on an old tandem, and with a fixed wheel at that.

At this time the A82 north was still a long, winding road. The vast improvements that were later to come on Loch Lomond-side were still on the drawing board. As the run to the Fort was quite long, the coach made a stop at the old Ben More tea rooms just east of Crianlarich. On reaching the Fort we had to change to another coach heading for Inverness. About a mile short of Fort Augustus we got off the bus and started out up a track which passed the nearby Cullachy House. Climbing all the way, and already with a long day's travel behind us, after four miles or so we reached a building named on the map as Blackburn. Here we set up our little tent, a cheap single-skin effort with no refinements. As we were settling down to eat, an ex-military-looking character appeared on a quad bike, obviously making sure we had not broken into the building to use it as a doss. As we were on the old Wade road and a right of way there was little he could say, so he simply left us to it.

Next morning, having camped at a fair height, we breakfasted and then set off into a misty landscape in our shorts and waterproof coats despite the damp. We were crossing a route steeped in history: Bonnie Prince Charlie and the great Montrose marched armies across the Corrieyarrick. Near to the summit of the Corrieyarrick Pass we met some shepherds: they would be the only people we saw that day. After descending the zigzags at the east end of the pass we finally dropped out of the mist and on to lower ground. A few miles further on, we reached a building marked on the map as Melgarve. We wondered why such a substantial building was left lying unlocked. There was some basic furniture so we were unsure if it was used or not. It was only much later that we found out that we had unwittingly visited our first bothy. We had a welcome rest and dried out with a fire, lit by Rab burning a pair of Japanese boots that had failed to come up to his expectations.

As the day was still young we decided to walk on. Soon the road beyond the old Garva Bridge improved – well, perhaps for cars, but not for us pounding steadily along on the hard tarmac. The miles rolled by as we followed the River Spey, still on Wade's route to Kingussie. As evening drew on we came to a part of the river that was dammed, forming a loch. We pitched the tent just up from the dam and spent a comfortable night's sleep in a bed of heather. Awaking to a fine morning we were soon on our way once more. This time we turned south into Strath Mashie, initially in forestry where we came upon a buzzard devouring its prey and oblivious to our presence. Soon we were back in more open country. Just south of Strath Mashie House we passed under the main Laggan-to-Spean Bridge road. A mile east, among rolling moorland with views to Kingussie up Glen Truim, we turned towards Dalwhinnie.

Passing low craggy hills to the north of the Fara we could see the pagodas of the Dalwhinnie distillery in the distance – the highest whisky distillery in the Highlands. Dalwhinnie was an important stopping-place for heavy-goods drivers. Sitting astride the main road just north of the Drummochter Pass it boasted a railway station, a couple of garages and two hotels, as well as a large transport cafe. One of the hotels – the old Grampian Lodge – I came to know well when I led walking holidays for the HF. When we reached the village we made straight for the village store and post office near to the Grampian. Here we stocked up on food, buying as much as we could afford and carry. Much refreshed and eager to be rid of civilisation once more, we walked the length of the one-street village to cross the river Truim.

Our route now took us east into the hills, but first we had to make our way across the new A9 – the road being built at that time that would by-pass Dalwhinnie, as it would many other hamlets, leaving them to wither on the vine. Once clear of the clutter of road construction we marched along on a hard hydro road leading up to Loch Cuaich. This road runs beside a large concrete overflow channel from the loch, which lies out of sight of the main roads, below the nearby Munro of Meal Cuaich. This was at a time when we were not focused on climbing Munros or we would probably have climbed the hill. Instead we walked to the far end of the loch and made camp among the heather. The nearby hydro-working had a plaque with the names of the men involved in the construction in the 1930s. On a dry but windy evening we lit a camp fire, but where we had camped it was difficult to sit near enough to get any heat without the wind blowing smoke into your face and freezing your back. Eventually we gave up and retired to the tent, thankful to crash out once more in the soft heather.

Next morning quite early we hit the trail again. This day I began to feel pain in my knees and I swapped my boots for soft trainers. On leaving the campsite we passed through a short but steep-sided pass and began to drop down into Glen Tromie. On reaching the river we crossed over a bridge onto a road that led us north and lower into the glen. Soon we were passing through the splendid woods of Glen Tromie.

Where the glen joins Strath Spey at Tromie Bridge the road turns west to the nearby ruins of Ruthven Barracks and the village of Kingussie. But we turned off into the hills and headed across-country through a mixture of woods and high heather moor. We were soon on a path that dropped us down into Glen Feshie near to Stronetopper. A horrible bulldozed road had recently been cut through the glen, once one of the most beautiful areas of natural woodland. Crossing the river not far from large locked gates, we passed the old bothy of Ruigh Aiteachain where Landseer is reputed to have visited and been inspired in painting his landscapes. As the splendid evening wore on we made camp a little farther up the glen under the pine trees just up from the river and lit a fire.

We set off early next morning. The pine trees of the glen soon gave way to high heather moorland. This was the watershed of several infant rivers: Feshie, Geldie and Eidart. The Eidart, which rises in the high moorland to the north, we had to cross. In time of spate this would be a difficult crossing but this fine morning it was just a dawdle. With the Ring of Tarf to our right and the Cairngorms dominating the rest of our view we crossed the highest point of the day's climb. In the distance across the moor we could see the old Geldie shooting lodge but were too far away to see anything other than a ruin. In time we came to an old building where the Geldie meets the route from Blair Atholl through the Glen Tilt. This building was just a ruin but still had a red corrugated tin roof so we called it the Red Hoose. Here we drummed up and made tea and something to eat. When we finished, one of us put the Dixies (square cooking pots) in the river, held down with a stone, to clean them. It was only miles later that we realised they had been left behind – for years after we blamed each other for their loss.

As we continued along a fair track on quite flat ground towards White Bridge I again began to suffer pain in my knee. When at last we fell out on the road at the Linn o' Dee we were really quite knackered, almost to the point of exhaustion. The Linn was in full spate with a foaming torrent of water roaring through its narrow gorge. Without a bridge over it the Linn must at one time been almost impossible to cross. Tourists in the early part of the nineteenth century reputedly crossed over a wobbly plank, and at one time in the 1930s a noted mountaineer, Menlove Edwards, actually swam through it for a dare. After the solitude of the past few days it felt unreal to be among what seemed like huge crowds. We lay about on the rocks beside the Linn for quite a while, basking in the warm sun. However, all too soon it was time to move on, and we staggered our way into Glen Luibeg. This was our first visit to the glen. At that time the approach to Derry Lodge was along a tree-lined stretch of road – the trees have sadly since been cut down. Once past Luibeg itself we made our weary way on a splendid evening to Corrour bothy. We camped outside the bothy – I don't remember why. Possibly we were too tired and too used to the tent by then, and the weather was good. But by now my knee was so painful I probably did not care where we slept that night.

Courrour bothy

When we awoke next morning we found that our camp in the Lairig was not getting the sun because of the steep hills all around. So we broke camp and staggered on. Crossing the Cairngorm bridge opposite the bothy we were soon back on the through path where we passed the spot known as the Tailors' Stone, where three Abernethy tailors perished while attempting to dance a reel at the dells of Abernethy, Rothiemurcus and Braemar within the space of twenty-four hours. Caught here in a ferocious Cairngorm blizzard on their way to the third dell they lost their lives. But a reel was the last thing on my mind as we began climbing up into the boulder fields at the summit of the pass. This part through the high pass of the Lairig was sheer agony for me hobbling along in a sea of pain. I was almost too engrossed in just trying to keep going to take in the wild scenery around us. The sun beat down as we emerged from the summit of the pass and out of the boulder fields. There the going became a little easier for me and on reaching the Sinclair Hut we had a welcome break. This hut, which I passed many times afterwards, was even then a dirty hovel and despite the heat of the day we were not inclined to linger very long. Our trail now began to drop into the Rothiemurchus Forest, which afforded pleasant shade from the hot sun as we sweated our way along a path covered in pine needles from the beautiful remnants of Caledonian pine forest. Where the path crossed the river over yet another Cairngorm club bridge we had a break and I bathed my sore feet in the crystal-clear, cold waters.

As we again moved on we knew that the end could not be far away but were surprised at just how quickly it did come. One minute I was staggering along in agony on an endless forest track and the next thing I knew, I had fallen out onto a main road with Rab shouting at me to run for a bus just getting ready to move off. Much to Rab's amusement I actually made a dash for it as if there had been nothing wrong with my knees at all. Thus ended our long walk – a hundred miles in five days, from Fort Augustus to Coylumbridge. I later found out that I had been suffering from a form of housemaid's knee, caused by work crawling about lofting boats.

'Nae quarters here, laddie!'

ONE DARK AND BRISK MORNING in the spring of 1975, Rab Doyle and I caught the early morning diesel at Dumbarton. Our plan was to walk cross-country north to south from Loch Rannoch to Crianlarich and on the way climb four – to us, remote – Munros. Disembarking at Rannoch station – as ever, on the side away from the platform to avoid any ticket collector – we caught the post bus along to the turn-off for Bridge of Gaur. A short walk along this wee road and we came to the old Rannoch barracks. We marched off past a gate with huge eagles on the posts, and promptly got lost. As usual if you don't get it right at the start it can all go wrong. So retracing our steps for about a quarter of a mile we soon got back on the correct heading and set off again.

Our first hill of the day was Meal Buidhe at the western end of Glen Lyon. Our approach was long and slow but the views behind us to the north were wide and unobscured by any hills; Loch Rannoch below us and the vast desert of the great moor of Rannoch lying away to the west. Meal Buidhe is one of those Munros that are probably only visited the one time. Years later the Gleniffer boys erected a black marble plaque with the names of past club members, with the added legend 'When will we see their likes again?' When indeed. As many of Scotland's glens lie west to east across the country, and with our route being north to south, there was much up and down work as we wound our way south. From Meall Buidhe we dropped off the hill down to Loch an Daimh.

This is a man-made loch and lies in a small glen which runs off Glen Lyon. When we reached the dam we sat at the bottom of it to have lunch. While we were basking here in the sun and enjoying the quietness we were suddenly blasted from our reverie by a pair of jet aircraft that had come from the west, skimming the loch at low level out of sight and sound till they flew over us sitting below the dam walls. We thought that the bloody dam above had burst as we jumped up in a blind panic.

From the dam we set off again to scale another remote Munro, Stuchd an Lochan. A steep pull up Coire Ban to a point marked at 987 metres took us onto the east–west ridge that forms the summit. Standing on the cairn we looked into the corrie with the small loch of Lochan nan Cat lying below us like a discarded

Peter on the slopes of
Ben Heasgarneach

slate. Further below was Loch An Damh and beyond again Meall Buidhe. Turning our backs to the way we had come we walked to the end of the ridge and slipped off the mountain down the long easy slopes of Meall an Odhar into Glen Lyon near the deserted village of Pubil. Here we would seek shelter for the night. Pubil was built to house some of the people who had lost their homes in the glen, swallowed up by the enlarged Loch Lyon when the dam was built.

Still a bit green about the ears, we went up to the door of a building that was occupied and asked if we could shelter somewhere that night. The wee man who came to the door was dressed in the kilt – a green tartan. Standing in the doorway, legs akimbo, arms folded, a smug grin on his face, he took great delight in informing us that, 'There will be no quarters in the glen for you tonight, laddies.' So much for Highland hospitality. His attitude brought to mind what Burns said on a visit to the Highlands: 'There's naething here but heilan pride, And heilan scab and hunger! If providence sent me here, 'Twas surely in an anger!'.

Well, undaunted and determined to get one over the little smug chap, we had a good scout around and not far below the hydro dam we found the local rubbish dump. In it was an old van. We settled down to doss in it for the night. From the rear windows we could see the wee keeper or whatever he was driving up and down the glen, obviously looking to see where we had gone. Despite being tired we slept badly that night, and not just because old wreck was lying at an angle. We were not the only occupants of the dump. The place was full of rats and it was a case of sleeping with one eye open. With first light about three o'clock we gave up on the idea of sleep. After rousing stiff limbs, and a meagre breakfast, we blearily crossed over the dam and headed up into the hills once more. The peak we were now headed for was Ben Heasgarneach (1,076 metres) or, as we translated into Glasgow-speak, 'Ben Hairy Arse'. Our route up Ben Hairy Arse was not quite direct; more of a weary meander up onto the ridge overlooking Coire Hesgairneach. It was still well before midday when we reached the summit. The weather had still been kind to us. A drop to the south and then south-west took us on to the last hill. Like Heasgarnich, Creag Mhor (1,047 metres) is a hill of broad grassy ridges and was climbed with relative ease. Instead of following the ridge round and into Glen Lochy we descended to the bealach that marks a watershed between Glen Lyon and Glen Lochy. From here we ascended onto a low part of the ridge on the Corbett of Cam Chreag and dropped straight into the head of Gleann a Chlachain under the looming mass of Ben Challum to our left. Very soon we had left the hills behind us, and emerged from Auch Glen into the more open and pastoral country that is Strath Fillan. Passing the old remains of the priory of Saint Fillan and crossing the bridge, we were all too soon on the main A82. Our progress slowed. Hoofing it along a hard tarmac road is not the best way to finish a long hike through the hills. Exhausted, we dropped off the road at a lay-by on the outskirts of Crianlarich. A drum-up and the last scraps of our food were needed to get us to the end. I lay down on the verge to rest while the water boiled. When Rab shook me awake for tea I was soaking. It had rained and I never even noticed.

The Glasgow HF

IN 1976 I JOINED THE Glasgow Holiday Fellowship. For many potential new members the name seemed off-putting. It suggested some sort of religious or temperance connection. In fact nothing could be further from the truth. Its members are a grand mixture from all walks of life. I was joining a club with a long history of going to the hills from before and throughout the great outdoor revolution of the inter-war years. It was formed during the time of the Great War by Thomas Arthur Leonard to encourage young people in the industrial heartland of northern England to enjoy the countryside. The Glasgow group was formed in 1917. At the time I joined them there were few club members who had climbed all the Munros. Going to the hills was combined with varied interests within the club. There were many active photographers, naturalists, birdwatchers. Munro-bagging at that time was not a highly regarded sport.

In the Holiday Fellowship – HF for short, sometimes known to members as 'Husbands Found' – I met wee Stukky Stirling. He was not long retired, and in his mid-sixties. Known to everyone as Stukky, the Scots name for a young starling, he was born in Kirkintilloch and as a child moved to Paisley. Before World War II he was an active member of the Johnstone Wheelers Cycling Club. He was a typical product of the hungry thirties – a natural-born scrounger. At a campsite or in a hostel he would appear just as the kettle began to boil with the words 'Is that a wee cuppa tea in the pot?' At the end of some outings he was often the recipient of any leftover food and rations that the rest of us would only throw away. He would say, 'This'll see me a wee stert fur ra week.'

His war service as a wireless telegraph operator in the Royal Navy took him from the heat of the tropics on convoy escort duty based at Bathurst near Freetown in West Africa, to the frozen wastes of the Russian convoys to Murmansk and Archangel. The ship he served on was HMS *Bergamot*, a Flower Class Corvette, the same type of ship as portrayed in the film *The Cruel Sea*. When the war was over he took the opportunity along with many other ex-servicemen to emigrate to Australia. Here he travelled around the bush country. On a large sheep station his task was to cut off the testicles of young lambs. After about six months or so he decided that this was a cruel thing to be doing and decided to move on – I wonder why it took so long? Years later, on a visit to Australia, he went to look up people he had stayed with. He was amazed to see that his racing bike was still hanging up in the old shed where he had left it. After a few years of wandering in Oz he returned to Scotland to live near his family in Paisley. Stukky eventually finished his working life when he retired from the Rootes car factory in Linwood. There he had become a member of the works climbing club named after the nearby Gleniffer Braes.

Although he was quite tough, like many of his generation he was blessed – or cursed, depending what way you looked at it – with a pig-headed stubborn streak and a brass neck. It was his pig-headedness that saw him through many of his long hard days in the hills. His legendary fiery short temper would on occasion rise to the surface and woe betide those in earshot. There was an occasion when the Gleniffer club were staying at a bothy where a lone Englishman was fruitlessly trying to light the fire using damp twigs. The rest of the guys, knowing what was coming, wisely kept out of the way. Able to contain himself no longer, into the bothy dived the wee man and within minutes the poor Sassenach was being driven down the glen, an irate Stukky snapping at his heels.

He was not a fast walker, just a steady plodder. Once he was walking he seldom ever stopped for a breather even when the rest of us were sprawled about grateful for a few minutes' rest. He would just say, 'Ah'll jist walk oan' and when we would set off we would find it hard to catch up with him. On one very rare occasion we were out on the mountains above Glen Doll and he was feeling the pace – he had not had much of a breakfast and had not taken enough food with him. As we stopped to let one of the lads catch up he just blew his top, ranting and shouting, 'Aye ye'll stoap fur him but no fur me!' Although well enough liked within the club, after a day on the hills he would lounge around in string vest and shorts. Perfectly acceptable when sunbathing at the Cloch Lighthouse by Gourock, but not quite so acceptable among the female company of the Holiday Fellowship in the evenings, especially the sight of his left testicle hanging loose from his shorts like a well-thumbed tobacco pouch.

His last big outing with the boys was to the Cairngorms. By now he had completed about 247 Munros. But the pain in his groin which earned him the nickname Stukky's Groin – after the hill Stuc a' Chroin – meant he eventually needed a hip-replacement operation. Although this was successful he began to suffer from clinical depression. It is likely that he could not cope with being inactive. He was taken into Erskine Hospital. He became a recluse and, as we say, adopted the foetal position and turned his face to the wall. When he died some of the lads erected a marble plaque on a mountain to him and another well-liked club member, Wee Wullie Young, who had recently also passed on. Wullie and Stukky were like chalk and cheese. You couldn't put the pair together in the one tent before they would start fighting and squabbling like a pair of bantam cocks. Wullie had been a sergeant during the war, one of the few survivors of the platoon he led on the D-day landings. So I was surprised at the pair on a plaque together. When I was first shown the plaque my comment was, 'We need a bigger one with room for more names!'

The Gleniffer

THE GLENIFFER WAS THE walking club of the old Rootes – latterly Chrysler – car manufacturing company of Linwood to the west of Paisley. Some of the car builders formed it when they worked in the 'factory'. The boys had the use of a works minibus for outings to the hills and an abundance of climbing equipment provided mainly by the company. In their early years they aspired to be real mountaineers – or maybe they just perspired to be. Often at club nights you could hear the cry, 'How aboot Y-gully fur a change?' Someone would reply, 'Aye, how fur why no?'

The leader of this club was the democratically unelected 'Preesident' George McCall. George originally came from Kilmarnock where he worked for the old farm tractor manufacturers Massey Ferguson, and spoke with a broad Ayrshire accent. In dodgy situations on the hill you would often hear him say, 'If Mergrit could see me noo,' or 'See yin boays, they wur werrin gey wat claes an wur gey gled tae hear sumdy speak English.' It was basically George who organised the Gleniffer outings, and he often took on the task of navigating. One of the things that sticks in my mind from when we climbed with the boys is that part of the fashion then was the wearing of heavy woollen tartan shirts. One night at a club meet George appeared dressed in a smart blue tartan shirt and was much admired by the rest of us. I innocently said to him that it was far too small for him and that it would fit me perfectly. George glared at me and proclaimed, 'Jist don't even think aboot it cause yer no gettin it, so there!' This despite the imminent danger that the buttons straining at his neck and stomach would part company with the material and put a few eyes out with flying missiles.

Bob Alexander (BA) was a stalwart member. He was a social worker and tended to take much of the stress of his job home with him. A sturdy good-looking guy with seemingly an ideal build for hillwalking, at times he lacked stamina despite looking generally fit and healthy. On a trip to Skye when George sat down exhausted, almost in tears, saying, 'Ma boattle's gone', Bob piped up, 'Aye, ma boattle's gone tae!' Yet only a short while later when the team were considering climbing the Basteir Tooth he was heard to say, 'Aye, ah'll dae it if you'll dae it tae!' Later that week when he was on part of the ridge on his own he saw a cairn and thought that it marked the way off. So down he went, only to find to his horror that he was on very steep ground, becoming steeper. Eventually he came upon a group of climbers below him on the way up. They were roped up with pitons and all the ironmongery. As they met, Bob blurted out, 'Y-you mu-must th-think that ah'm fucking d-daft, b-but how th-the fuck dae ye get doon oot o here?' The heavily armoured climbers could only reply, 'Nivver mind us – how the bloody hell did you get up there?'

All of us in the Gleniffer are indebted to Bob Alexander. If it was not for him none of us would have ever finished the Munros. It was Bob who enlisted the services of a qualified climbing instructor who took us all to the Whangie out by the Queen's View to learn how to abseil and climb using ropes. Scottish pride, and Paisley frugality, prevented us from hiring the services of a guide. There was no way any of us were going to pay some wee Englishman to judge if we were fit for the Cuillins and to pay for the privilege of being lowered off the Inaccessible Pinnacle like a sack of potatoes. Jimmy (The Galloper) Gallagher came from the village of Bridge of Weir in rural Renfrewshire. He was a bit of a rebel in the car factory, occasionally clashing with George, who was his gaffer, over rates for piecework. Jimmy took the closure of the car factory very much to heart. Feeling bitterly betrayed, it was as if 'the system' was out to get him personally. He was quite rightly regarded as a big hero in the club, being the first of the Gleniffer and one of the first in the HF to complete the Munros. But after he came out on a few outings with Rab and I we got the impression that Jimmy was in reality rather timid on the hills. On one memorable occasion after a huge day on the Strathfarrar hills he lay exhausted beside the road. Rab was surprised to hear him sigh, 'Oooh, that wis a big day.' Since then Rab was annoyed that

I never heard Jimmy utter defeat like that as I had dropped behind almost at the end of the walk, ravenously chewing on a heel of dry bread. Jimmy was always getting hill names wrong. Tom Dhuibh would become 'Tam Dub'; Maol Bhuidhe, 'Mole Buddie'; Outliers, 'Outliners'. Jimmy eventually disappeared from the climbing club scene and went on to tackle the Corbetts, seemingly preferring his own company and to all intents eventually became very much a recluse. Big (The Joker) Malky originally came from Linthouse. This of course automatically disqualified him from being a Govanite. Still, Al was well enough liked despite this drawback. Big Malky became in all probability the world's most travelled french polisher. Preesident George, who had taken Big Malky under his wing, called him a 'learnin boay'. He worked for the Ministry of Defence. Wherever there was a far-flung outpost of the British Empire, Big Malky would be there, french-polishing the tables in the officers' mess. It was always comforting to know that if we ever went to war, Big Malky would be there as our first line of defence, polishing off the enemy. He visited far-off places such as St Kilda and the Falklands, and rather bizarrely when at the British Embassy in Warsaw he brought back photographs of the ovens at Auschwitz. On a trip to St Kilda he was invited to a 'medieval night' in the sergeants' mess. When he awoke the next morning he was suffering from a hangover and covered in chicken grease. Maybe he shouldn't have gone as a serving wench.

Malky was a prolific joke-teller with an endless repertoire of totally unfunny jokes. He also had the most unnerving habit of continually turning round to talk to his terrified passengers while he was driving. On one occasion as we headed west along the Laggan road to climb one of the Monadhliath hills he was talking away to us in the rear when suddenly he lost control of the car on a bend. From the middle of the back seat with Rab and Stukky I had a grandstand slow-motion view as the car spun out of Mal's control on loose gravel and shot through a fence, becoming airborne for a short time. I could see that the top strand of wire had not parted and thought we would all be decapitated. As we flew through the air we landed heavily in a sloping stony field and began to slide at an alarming rate towards a steep drop over-looking a fast-flowing river far below. Miraculously the car ground to a bone-jarring halt just yards from disaster. Big Malky was vainly trying to start the thing and gibbering, 'It's alright, ah'll jist get it started ah wull.' I could not quite figure out how, because the wheels and exhaust were scattered about the field behind us. As it was, I was shouting 'Let me oot' and shoving a dazed Stukky out the door, fearing that the car was going to explode. A young couple who were working on a house nearby and had seen us crash helped us up to the house where they kind-ly gave us tea and let some of us change our trousers before giv-ing us a run into Kingussie where we caught the service bus home. I never told the wife about the crash till weeks after. Malky never told as many jokes again. After all they were nearly the death of us. Chris (The Handsome One) Barclay, a native of Renfrew, was almost the same age as myself. He always was a pretty fit guy and extremely handsome (in Rab Doyle's view). On the hills he would run up and down like a sheepdog with endless energy while the rest of us struggled at our best pace. For much of the time he had absolutely no sense of direction and if you followed him, both of you would get lost. I had a theory that to go to the hills one had to be either extremely fit or just plain daft in the heid. Chris worried me on this idea as he seemed to wander back and forth across this border-line with comparative ease. On one occasion on the Carn Marig hills, Chris met a guy who made the mistake of telling him that he was a brain surgeon. Chris may well have been a bit of a hypochondriac, always thinking he had some ill-ness, real or imaginary, so meeting a medical person on the hills was too good an opportunity for him to miss.

Jackie (Kenwood) Harrison from the town of Johnstone was the club's official sage and flyman who knew all the angles. A heavy smoker, he was the supposed keeper of the club records – the infa-mous 'Doomsday Book' that chronicled the club's misadventures and disasters. He was known as Kenwood for stirring up gossip. Jackie was one of the first to suffer ill health, in the form of a heart attack on the hills, and for a while afterwards it seemed few would be keen to accompany him. On one occasion when he tripped over a gate and we went to help him up he started to get rather shirty: he thought we were trying to strip him of his Goretex gear. It became a standard joke that if one dropped dead the others could fight over the spoils.

Shughie (The Poacher) was the real flyman of the club. He was the big game hunter who knew someone who knew someone else who was in the famous Creag Dubh climbing club. Shughie bore a striking resemblance to his boxer dog: he brought to mind the expression 'A face like a rat catcher's dug'. Shughie realised too late that he had missed out on the big game of Munro-bashing and that the 'poacher' image that he had carefully cultivated over the years had all been a wasted effort. Andra (The High Plains Rifter) Murdoch was a quiet, lean, easy-going guy who never said much at the best of times and has been a stalwart of the club since it began. His best-known saying was 'Hiv ye goat ra bearin?' I would usually reply in consternation, 'Aye, ah've goat four bairns at hame!' Last but not least was Hamish the bin-lorry driver, a small guy who was, if possible, even worse-looking than Hughie's dog. He was what could only be described as a 'bar-room mountaineer'. He appeared from nowhere one club night armed with all sorts of Munro Tables and guidebooks at a time when we had all just about nearly finished the Munros anyway. He suffered from verrucas on both feet and could hardly walk any distance.

Rab Doyle and myself enjoyed many memorable camping weekends and climbed many memorable Munros with the boys, as a club and in groups. Jimmy Galloper and Stukky Stirling were also members of the Glasgow HF club. On my first few outings with the boys I had to make my way across the Clyde to Paisley very early some mornings: they met near the Gilmour Street Station at the ungodly hour of five. (The Paisley men believed in getting the most out of a day.) On some outings I had farther to walk getting to and from pick-up points than the day's walk on the hills. Not long after, when most of us had finished our Munros and were considering what we should do from then on, I suggested that the English Lake District might make a nice change. This was faced by a stony silence from the team till at last Andra replied, 'Aye, but whit urr we gonnae dae in the efternoon?' It would only be fair to mention that Rab Doyle and I were paid-up members of the Gleniffer for a few years until our membership lapsed and we became the 'dishonorary members from the north bank'. There always seemed to be some sort of cultural difference between us 'Glesga keelies' and the 'Paisley men'. While we were content to waste a day in travelling to faraway hills and do the same on the way home, they on the other hand went out of their way to make their outings very much 'cost-effective'. Meals were another area of our different cultural outlook. On the hills or in bothies, the boys stuck to cooking with ancient smelly paraffin primus stoves long after most folk had adopted cleaner disposable gas cartridges. Many of their meals were basic, such as mince and tatties prepared at home, while we carried all sorts of dishes made on the hills.

Often on the way home Doyle and I went into hotels for pub lunches while for years the highlight of the Gleniffers' journey home would be a stop at Auchterarder for a fish supper. Another difference between us was that, while many of the lads pursued their various careers, at times I think they might have viewed us as a pair of 'wasters' – I suppose because of Rab having worked very little of his adult life and me having endured prolonged spells of unemployment, a particular hazard of boat building. The biggest disappointment for us was the way the lads celebrated finishing their last Munros. With the exception of Bob Alexander they were simply day outings and not the drunken overnight session we had for our last one.

Easter at Braemar

ONE EASTER WEEKEND RAB and I joined an HF Easter club outing to the Cairngorm Mountains with Braemar youth hostel as our base. It was organised by a bloke in the Glasgow HF, Duncan Livingstone. Duncan was a really nice wee guy, always cheerful, a real character and a well-liked member of the club. Tragically he and his wee wife were brutally murdered by his own son in a drunken rage. This was a memorable trip as it was the outing that introduced Rab Doyle to the club. From the hostel at Braemar in typical chilly weather for this place we walked smartly along to Glen Callater and then up into the right of way of 'Jock's Road'. We climbed the Munro of Carn Saigart Mhor and from there went on to the summit of Lochnagar. It was a day of sunny spells, with deep snow, and occasionally visibility was wiped by wild snow squalls. On the top at the cairn we quickly posed for a few photos while it was clear, then we turned back on a bearing before another snow squall wiped out the view. At one point as we descended Rab thought he would be smart and went off to take in a nearby top. As he did so he lost sight of the party in a squall and almost got himself completely lost.

I don't remember much of our time in the hostel then except how cold Braemar can be, but the next day we bussed along to the Linn of Dee. There we walked out to the White Bridge and returned by way of the Lairig Ghru and into Glen Luibeg on a big circular walk. This was where wee Stukky and Rab first met. Wee Stukky asked, 'How long huv you known Peter?' Much to Stukky's annoyance Rab's reply was that he had known me for over ten years as to the wee man's two. This might have seemed a strange thing for Stukky to ask anyone. However when you got to know him you would realise that he was a compulsive collector of names and addresses of people he met on his travels. At times on trips to Australia and New Zealand it was a useful means of board and lodgings. Before the party reached the Lairig we walked up past the impressive rain-swollen Chest of Dee. It was near here we stopped for lunch and one of the party, a wee German lady, Trudi, gave everyone Easter eggs to roll. The way

Rab and Peter at Cairnwell on the way to Braemar

through the pass to Rothiemurchus was blocked by heavy snow and we had our work cut out just walking by the river. In the Fife Arms Hotel later that day we heard that the Army had tried to send a party through the pass the night before but had been forced to retreat back to Coylumbridge. We had walked fifteen miles that day despite the heavy-going in snow: I had felt fine but had begun to have a niggling pain in my knee. The last time I had such bother was on our earlier long-distance walk from Fort Augustus to Coylumbridge. Were the Cairngorms a jinx on me? I had to wonder. When we returned to the hostel that night I was hardly able to stand on it and it was with great difficulty that I managed to make it to the Invercauld Hotel.

Braemar hostel would see us return on many future visits. On one of these later stays, as we were being driven up in a coach, the driver nearly took us to Braemar instead of Glen Doll hostel and it was only after a heated argument he was persuaded to deliver the party to the correct destination. The driver, who was no walker and rather overweight, was only interested in having a few pints before bed and subsequently his snoring kept some of us awake most of the night. There can be nothing worse than being deprived of sleep after hard days on the hills. The next day the whole party walked through to Braemar over 'Jock's Road'. It was near the shelter, Davy Glen's Bourach, that we met another HF member, John Cameron, coming the opposite way carrying his push-bike. When we reached Braemar that night we went to the hotel and so did the driver. When we had to go back for lights-out at the hostel he decided to remain in the bar. Very late he arrived back at the hostel banging on a window to get in. Once inside, instead of going to sleep, he sat up guzzling crisps and drinking Irn-Bru. Finishing all this he lay on his back and immediately began to snore loudly. I could handle no more. I needed my sleep and was prepared to kill for it. Creeping as stealthily as I could I sneaked over to his bunk and slowly pulled the duvet cover off him. If I wasn't getting a sleep, neither was he. He had

Loch Callater on Jock's Road

a very bad night's sleep: he woke up but couldn't find the duvet, which I had shoved under another bed. It did not stop him on the last night again going to the pub and banging on a window in the early hours to be let in. That same night an old guy of dubious age had booked into the now busy hostel. He was certainly no walker or climber, more like some old tramp, in an old threadbare pin-striped suit, obviously looking for a night under a roof. During the evening we were puzzled to see him taking a long time removing the lid of a very large tin, but as he bothered no one we thought no more about him till the following morning. As usual in the hostel everyone was up early frantically packing gear away and getting ready for the day's climb and the journey home – everyone, that is, except our inebriate coach driver snoring away in the corner bunk. Suddenly from the opposite corner, heading slowly for the door, comes the old-timer delicately holding his large tin – now full to the brim with urine. At the sight and smell, bodies quickly parted to let him pass. It dawned on a few of the lads what was going to occur. Concentrating on his can of piss the old boy failed to see a rucksack on the floor in his way. The inevitable happened. As if in slow motion he tripped and as people dived for cover the can of warm pee flew from his precarious grip and splashed all over the sleeping driver.

However, back then on our first visit to this hostel the problem that kept me awake was my painful knee. So when we departed the next morning I had decided not to go with the others on the climb before we drove home. On arriving at the busy ski centre at Glen Shee just down the road from Braemar, the party set off in sunshine and deep snow to climb Glas Maol. Feeling very disappointed I set off to try and climb up the skiers' hill of Cairnwell. About halfway up the hill my knee became too sore to continue, so I abandoned the climb. It had also started snowing heavily and visibility was only a few yards. As I struggled down I had an idea. I was hobbling along just below the ski lift and at one point I found that I could jump up and cadge a free descent off the hill. So that is what I did. When I met up with Rab and the others back at the bus it seemed that they too were unable to reach their top. But we would be back another day.

Munro Bashers

THE YEAR 1982 WAS without doubt the most productive that we ever had in all our time on the hills. Like many others who should have known better, we eventually got ourselves caught up on the dreadful Munro treadmill. These days everybody and their granny has done the Munros, and quite rightly – it is a great personal achievement that many people can do if fairly fit. Rab and I like to pride ourselves that there was never any doubt about what we did. There were no misgivings that we might have missed tops in bad weather, and no other reasons for uncertainty. With many of the large groups of hills that we went into, we stayed there till we had done them. There were no 'kirby grips', as Rab called them – straight up and down with a kick at the cairn. All in, it took us about twenty years to complete them. We had no reason to do them again

The peak of Peter's yacht-building years: *Justine III*

so we moved on to other things. The best thing that came from the Munros was the unknown and isolated corners of Scotland they took us to. To finish them off and put them behind us we had taken a break from our long-distance walks. It was out-and-out Munro-bagging at its worst. For most of 1982 and beyond, Rab and I teamed up with members of the HF to hammer away at the Munros – with Big John McEwan, Derek Sakol, Irene Cook, Pat

75

Wright and Susan Fyfe – and for the remainder we teamed up with the Gleniffer boys.

In the midst of this climbing activity we were shocked by the sad loss of a young friend of mine and member of the HF. His name was Robert: he and I had been going to the hills at a time when Rab Doyle had been away planting trees. On a weekend when I had been away with Stukky Stirling and Cathy Macmillan from the HF, Robert had gone climbing on the Cobbler, one of our early favourites. With a cine camera he had followed climbers up the south peak and there he fell to his death. We heard the news naming him as we drove home down Loch Lomond. It was over twenty years later before I went back up the Cobbler. I felt for a long time that if I had not gotten caught up with Munro-bagging I might have been with him that day and with a different outcome. He was only 21 when he died.

After that, almost every week we were pounding away at the big hills and during that year we climbed seventy-two Munros, seventeen tops and one single Corbett. On the Easter weekend we wiped out seventeen Munros in the Glen Shiel area. These included the Clunie Ridge and the Five Sisters of Kintail. On another trip to Loch Lochy youth hostel we had a huge day on the Meall an Teanga hills on the west side of the Great Glen. Around midsummer we all traversed the Aonach Eagach ridge. This we did from the bottom of the Devil's Staircase at Altnafeadh, all the way to the Pap of Glencoe to finish at the Clachaig Inn. The Blackmount, Loch Tay, Mamores and many other Munros fell to our assault that year. Yet this was no great achievement. Greater numbers of hills have been climbed by others in much shorter periods and in other more spectacular parts of the world. What made our big days on Scotland's mountains and glens so special to us was that we were continuing the traditions of working-class climbers and walkers in a sport that has nowadays reverted to what it originally was, a middle-class pastime. It was done at a time when I was also very active in my career as a yacht builder. For most of the years I went to the hills I was also raising a growing family and forging a reputation as one of Scotland's top custom racing yacht builders. The spring of 1982 also saw the peak of my yacht-building career. We were working hard building a One Ton yacht for an Irishman. Called *Justine III*, that same year it became the top boat in the World One Ton Cup yachting series, and it achieved an unbeaten record number of wins in the history of the series. I am quite proud that it still stands today.

Glenfinnan

AS 1983 BEGAN I experienced great changes in my circumstances. In the space of a year I had gone from being at the vanguard of high-tech yacht building to a bleak and uncertain future facing life on the dole. In desperation, broke, and with my wife expecting another child, I was forced onto a job-creation project for unemployed people. I had worked with some of the others there in the past. We were charged with the task of refurbishing an old fifty-odd foot, two-masted yacht used for underprivileged children. The vessel had been under construction in Holland just prior to the outbreak of war in 1939. It had been completed by forced labour, but whoever they were they knew little or nothing about boat construction and by now she was in a sorry state. Now here we were, some of us highly skilled and down on our luck, working as forced labour, victims of Thatcher's policies. As the job progressed we began to realise just how unscrupulous the people in charge were. Day after day people were verbally abused and harangued, and sacked at will.

Despite this I kept making plans for the hills. The idea was to head for Knoydart at Easter. It looked as if the Army were set to purchase the Knoydart peninsula and bar the public from access. Situated right on the west coast, Knoydart is one of the few areas of the Highlands that retain even today their ancient isolation. A place where even Johnny Wade and his successors never penetrated with their roads.

Straight from where I was working in Glasgow I caught the 4.35 Mallaig train with Rab at Queen Street Station. Many hill-walkers were making a massive invasion before access was restricted. Our five-day walk started from Glenfinnan station on a dark night into unknown territory to look for Corryhully bothy. In pitch darkness, with no moon, we slowly padded under the brooding Glenfinnan viaduct with our heavy packs. Our breath hung in the cold night air as we laboured up the glen with knees almost buckling under our loads. Looking for an unlit dark building set back from the trail on a dark night was not an inspiring start to a trek in a part of the country we had never been to. We were startled by something rushing by to our right: red deer that we had spooked were running up and down a deer fence trying to get away from us.

It was a sheer stroke of luck that we found the bothy in the darkness, with an enormous sense of relief. To miss finding it would have had serious consequences in such a barren area. Corryhully then was just an empty building with nothing in the way of furnishings. No table seats or sleeping platform, just a bare dirt floor with a dirty old mattress and an old broken fireplace. When you lay on your back and looked up at the old tin roof it had holes which you could see the stars through. But we had found the place and were glad to find it unoccupied. By torchlight we had a bite to eat and soon settled down on the dirt floor in our sleeping bags. Sometime later in the wee small hours I was wakened by someone banging on the door. At first I thought Rab had gone outside and had locked himself out, so in my sleepy state I gave him a shove and told him to get up and let himself in. When he grunted that he was not in fact outside at all but lying on the floor I had to get up and open the door. Prancing around a cold bothy in bare feet is not a nice experience. The door-bangers were a crowd of English guys who had just driven up from the Midlands or some place. Grudgingly we let them in and soon all settled down for the night.

Next morning Rab and I just got up and left to venture up the glen to our two hills for the day. It was dry but bleak low down: the tops were well covered with snow. Sgurr Na Coireachain and Sgurr Thuilm were a hard climb. With full packs we plodded round them in soft, deep snow. Visibility was just enough to navigate our way. There was a huge gash which gouged into the side of the mountain; because of deep overhanging snow cornices it would have been a real danger if visibility had been worse.

On descending we found ourselves on the wrong ridge, but this was no real problem. We could see to our right the end of Loch

Arkaig and the old buildings at Strathan where there was an old school-house. To the left was Glen Pean and Pean bothy; in front of us, Glen Dessary and A'Chuil bothy. After a cold river-crossing in bare feet we bypassed Strathan and walked round to A'Chuil bothy where we met up with some friends from the Glasgow HF.

A'Chuil wasn't just busy, it was jumping. By force we gained

Rab preparing to leave Corryhully

occupation of a small room in the middle of the building. Later, as others arrived and the bothy filled to bursting, some camped outside while others made improvised shelters with building material that had been brought in for renovation work. The evening was spent trying to crowd round the meagre fire with all sorts of bothy bums holding forth noisily, trying to outdo one another.

Next morning it was hard to rise early after a night sleeping on a hard floor. Outside, more people had arrived overnight and they were camped everywhere. Due to these huge numbers all heading for the bothy in Knoydart we decided to alter our plans and instead head for the bothy in Glen Kingie, Kinbreak. The day being sunny, dry and fairly mild and we had an easy walk over the pass in snow to Kinbreack. Arriving at the bothy we spent some time cutting down rafters from a nearby building and soon had a good fire going. In the evening more arrived and with drink being passed around a noisy night ensued till we all turned in around one in the morning. Despite the late night we were up at six-thirty. We relit the fire and were away for nine. After wading the river we had a walk along the glen to climb Gairich, another Munro, from the bealach. From the tops we had views of snow-clad mountains in all directions, while to the south-east we could clearly see the humpback shape of Ben Nevis. Our descent off the east ridge was to prove quite difficult. Once on the glen floor we had a break. After we had walked a bit further I discovered that I had left my camera so I just about-turned and went back for it. I found it sitting on a rock where I had left it.

As we came down the glen, the fine day soon gave way to heavy snow showers and falling temperatures. Re-crossing the river was unpleasant, having to wade barefoot and run the short distance to the bothy. However, it was occupied by our friends Irene, Susan and Alistair who had a fire going. I can always remember some-one giving me a hot drink which I drank straight from the pan, not noticing that I was scalding hands and mouth. We spent another merry night which was less noisy than the previous one because there was no drink left.

The next morning we woke up after another night on a hard floor to find that there was a deterioration in the weather. It had snowed heavily overnight and was looking very bleak. Rab and I were now low on provisions and the dried food we had been eating was going straight through us.

Everyone in the bothy was of the same opinion, and so it was a large party that made its way back over the pass to Glen Dessary. With snow now at low levels the sun came out to give stunning views of the mountains. Upon reaching Strathan everyone packed up in cars and left. Before doing so we were given a whip-round of everyone's remaining food and proceeded to indulge in a large drum-up beside the River Dessary in the sun.

Crossing two rivers, Dessary and Pean, we had a long slow trek over the pass between the Streaps and Sgurr Thuilm. Late in the afternoon in fading light we arrived back at Corryhully. After chatting briefly to a couple of guys who were passing through, we lit up a huge fire. With the last remnants of our food we made a meal and had a jolly evening with the bothy to ourselves, feeling quite pleased – masters of the glen, flushed with the success of the past few days. Waking early next morning with the fire now out

Kinbreack bothy

and the bothy bleak and cold we had a meagre breakfast of boiled trail-mix, coffee, bread and butter. With the bothy swept and us packed up we hoofed it out to Glenfinnan. As we got to the village, the butcher's van and the baker's van were just leaving in opposite directions. Rab and I chased one each till they stopped and sold us some sausages and rolls. With these spoils we had a disgusting but great greasy fry-up in the station waiting room. When I finally got home after ten, I had a cuppa tea and fell asleep. We had climbed three Munros, walked into three glens – Finnan, Dessary and Kingie – and had four uproarious nights in three bothies – Corryhully, A'Chuil and Kinbreck.

Within a few days of our return from Glenfinnan I was sacked from my job. This was not really a surprise to me. The way the project was being run, it was simply a matter of time before it was my turn. However, as we say in boat building, 'As wan door closes anither wan slams in yer face'; a few days later I was away at sea with my old friend Bill McKay delivering a motor boat to Norwich, and this itself was to prove quite an adventure.

Inverkip to Lymington

ON A GREY AND DISMAL afternoon I helped to cast off the mooring lines of the motor yacht White Bear at Kip Marina on the Firth of Clyde. I was helping Bill MacKay, an old friend and well-known Scottish yachtsman, and his friend Willie Kerr from Edinburgh. We were tasked with delivering a large Taiwan trawler motor boat to new owners in Ipswich. As we cleared the marina and moved out into the Firth it was a strange feeling to be sailing past the familiar outline of the hills of Arran. With a weak sun setting in the west and Ailsa Craig slipping astern of us, we sailed on into the Irish Sea. With only three of us on board we set out watch duties: this meant that Willie and I could get our heads down before our turn at the wheel. However, that first night at sea, trying to sleep in the aft cabin, I began to suffer really horrible sea-sickness. These boats are quite good sea boats and do not let much water come over the bow, but in any sea they roll and pitch wildly and in the aft end I was being thrown about all over the place. For that first night and into the next day I spent much of the time in the toilet being sick at both ends till nothing was left to bring up. This condition, common to those who over-indulge in strong drink, is usually known as 'the dry boak'. I was completely helpless and unable to take my turn on deck, leaving Bill to sail the boat single-handed, as even Willie in the fore end was suffering too. As we ploughed into the oncoming seas Willie was thrown against the deck-head banging his head. As the second day wore on and we crept slowly south, the seas moderated and after taking some sea-sickness tablets I found in my bag I began to feel much better.

With a set course to steer I was able to take my turn at the wheel while Bill got his head down and caught up on some much-needed sleep. Although we had some food with us, apart from not feeling like eating we could only make some hot drinks. Our course south was uneventful. I only had to steer clear of the few fishing vessels working across our course. For most of that day the distant coast of Ireland lay off our starboard side, and with the Isle of Man now slipping far astern of us the others were feeling better for a good sleep. As the light began to go the sea got rough again, yet still we plodded on at a steady ten knots. We were now off the coast of Wales in the broad expanse of Cardigan Bay. This was when the engines began to give us problems. Up till now they had droned away without a murmur. Without warning they began to splutter and falter. As we lost way Bill went down below for a look to see what the problem was. The engine-room – below the wheelhouse in this type of vessel – was deafening, cramped, very hot, and stank of diesel. I could not spend time there without feeling ill, so I was kept on the wheel trying to face the boat into the wind while Bill struggled to find out what was wrong. He was unable to locate the trouble but by dismantling and cleaning the fuel filters on each engine in turn he kept them going till they acted up again and again. Our speed had dropped by half. A decision was made to make for the nearby port of Fishguard to seek shelter. In the early hours of the morning we limped into the harbour, hooked up to a mooring close to the ferry terminal, and gratefully crawled into our bunks as the boat rocked us gently to sleep in the sheltered port. The next morning, after a futile attempt to sort the engines, Bill decided that we should set off once more. After picking up the hook we cleared the harbour and headed west past the rough-looking point of Strumble Head. After a few hours on a south-westerly course we turned south to pass Ramsey Island and sail across St Brides Bay. By now the weather was making a turn for the worse. The shipping forecast for the sea area we were in was predicting gales and we were slap-bang in the middle of it. In a very short time mounting green seas, which seemed in our tiny craft to be as high as houses, were tossing the vessel around. Willie was almost permanently down below keeping the engines running. Bill was strapped in at the wheel and I had jammed myself against the middle of the main bulkhead in the wheelhouse next to the radio behind Bill.

I had never been to sea in such conditions before and was ignorant of how serious it might become, but I could see that Bill was worried. As we plunged madly up and down towering green walls it was lucky for us that little or no water was being shipped over the bows. However, we corkscrewed and pitched badly from side to side. The curtains in the wheelhouse stood horizontally from the side. Drawers shot across the deck spilling their contents everywhere. As our little vessel battered into the seas, we heard a loud banging from outside. The inflatable life-raft just aft of the wheelhouse had broken loose and was in danger of being washed overboard. It would have been foolish to lose a means of safety in such extreme conditions. With no other option, Bill motioned Willie and me to go out and secure it. As we grabbed waterproofs I was terrified at the prospect of going out on the deck because we had no lifejackets and any slip would be fatal. As we opened the sliding door the wind ripped our breath away, plucking at us as we held on for dear life and edged our way aft. The seas were coming over the low thwarts and railing. It was definitely a case of one hand for the ship and the other for yourself. In the far distance we could see through squalls of rain the forbidding cliffs of the island of Skomer and its neighbour Skokholm. The wind by now was screaming in the rigging and each wave we topped was whipped away in driving spray. Very quickly – yet it seemed like slow motion – we secured the raft and fought our way back into the wheelhouse.

On passing Skokholm, Bill turned us east and we began to run with the wind behind us. We were fortunate that the boat was carried along at speed, otherwise the heavy seas would have swamped us from astern. Bill had decided to run for shelter in Milford Haven, where we could glimpse a huge tanker every time we crested a wave.

Milford Haven as we entered it did not look much of a haven. It was only when we slipped into Angle Bay that the wind dropped. As there were quite a few yachts moored here we decided to anchor till the storm blew over. That evening I tidied up the boat and cooked a meal, the first real food we had tasted since leaving the Clyde (I was to learn later that Bill was not known for feeding his crews). I awoke the next morning aware that something was not quite right. Then it came to me: the boat was lying over at an acute angle and not moving at all. On looking out the porthole we saw that we had anchored in a shallow bay that completely dried out at low tide. Bill was mortified. He had never run aground in all his sailing career. And worse: all the boats moored around us were sitting upright on twin keels. Although the storm had passed we had to sit and wait patiently until there was enough water under the keel before we could proceed.

When we eventually cleared Milford and left Wales astern, our course took us across the mouth of the Bristol Channel. With clearer skies and a rolling swell we took turns on the wheel, occasionally conning the boat from the flying bridge above the wheelhouse. With improving weather and no land in sight things settled down to a boring routine as we nursed the boat along. I stayed awake that night till we rounded Land's End and entered the English Channel before turning in. Our last full day at sea was a long, boring haul up the Channel. Sometimes steering from the flying bridge we could see just how busy the Channel is. I was surprised at the many large ships that forged past as if we weren't there. Scanning them through binoculars we could see no sign of life on some of them. I was glad we were not in mid-Channel at night. We were still only off Portland Bill when I again turned in, and when I woke in the early hours we had stopped engines. I could see that we were close inshore off a large town with what looked like an oil rig framed against the shore. We were looking at the lights of Bournemouth from Poole Bay, and Bill was tying to fix our exact position. He had decided to terminate the trip at Lymington, a small Hampshire yachting centre. In the pre-dawn light we entered the western approach to the Solent. On our starboard side we could see the white shapes of the Needles and the lighthouse with the Isle of Wight behind. Following a line of poles sticking out from the surrounding mudflats, we wound our way slowly up the Lymington river. It was almost broad daylight as Bill stood on the flying bridge, conning the boat into the marina and heading for the nearest pontoon while Willie and I took up positions on the deck ready to jump ashore and tie her up. Bill was shouting for us to land but from where he was he could not see that it was too far for me to jump. When we did get tied up we had a few hours' sleep before heading ashore to look for food. After days at sea I found it difficult to walk on terra firma as we headed into Lymington town. This voyage was at an end but I would return to Lymington quite a few times in the future.

Laggan Locks to Inverie

THIS WAS A LONG-DISTANCE walk from the Laggan Locks of the Caledonian Canal in the Great Glen westwards to the sea at Inverie, taking in six fairly remote Munros, camping high in the mountains and several bothies – Garrygulloch, Kinbreack, Sourlies – and Inverie hostel. Four hot, blistering days of hard walking with insufficient food saw us approaching the tiny hamlet of Inverie exhausted and starving. Speaking of food, for many years Rab always insisted on carrying most of our foodstuff while I carried my heavy old SLR cameras and an assortment of lenses. It took a few years for the penny to drop that while his pack got lighter mine always stayed the same.

When we set off on the Uig bus on this trip in July we met Flo McPhail, an old friend from the HF. She must have been horrified at the pair of us weighed under with our enormous packs. At Laggan Locks we got off the coach and went into the canal-side cafe for lunch. About three-thirty on a hot afternoon we set off walking west, heading for Knoydart. Soon we found ourselves sweating under a relentless sun on a long, hot, dusty road, hemmed in by miles and miles of dense forestry and pursued by hordes of bloodthirsty clegs. For some strange reason they seemed to prefer Rab's blood to mine. As was normal at the start of many of our walks we promptly got ourselves lost and to rectify our mistake we had to make a wide detour towards the River Garry. This mistake actually proved fortunate as we came to a pony-trekking centre at a place called Garrygulloch. Here was a remarkable bothy with bunks and mattresses and, best of all, we had the place to ourselves – that is, except for a large cat and a family of Dutch people who were on a pony-trekking holiday from Garrygulloch to Inverie. We would come to meet these people almost daily.

Early next morning it was shoulder packs and off into the west again. Our track followed along the River Garry which, due to the lack of recent rain, was very low and smelly. We eventually parted company with the river and turned into Glen Kingie, and here the burning sun beat down on us once we cleared the forestry. We thankfully reached the ruined building at Lochan before walking along the south side of Gairich. Here we took the chance to drum up and get out of the sun for a while. Before we

Peter in Garrygulloch bothy

left we carved our names on the wall – the gratuitous graffiti 'Kemp and Doyle 1982'. It was our intention to camp on the bealach between Gairich and our first Munro. However, soon after we made camp and tried to settle down for the night it became horribly obvious that the midges were getting into the tent through a small vent. After futile attempts to repel them and with Rab on the verge of insanity we hurriedly abandoned camp. The tent was thrown into bags and like a pair of demented loonies we made a run for it. The nearest shelter was Kinbreak bothy and as the river was low we ran right through it and made straight for the bothy, dispensing with the usual barefoot river-crossing. Kinbreak, unlike on our last visit, was thankfully empty that night except for us. After a bad sleep on the hard floor we set off later than usual. Stiffly we retraced our steps to the bealach of the previous night and very slowly we climbed up and over the two Munros of Sgurr Mhor and Sgurr Nan Choireachain. Despite another dry, warm day, the tops were pleasantly cool with good views and visibility. Just beyond the second mountain of the day, with a fine sunset over the Knoydart hills and glimpses of Skye and the islands, we made camp on the col at about 1,000 metres. Well above the dreaded midges, we had a good night's sleep up high and under the stars.

Surrounded by a damp, clinging, swirling mist we woke early. A meagre breakfast saw the last of our bread. Breaking camp, the tent soaked in condensation, we lazily daundered along the ridge; at first in mist, but soon this began to clear away as if some hand had pushed aside a curtain. Ahead, our path followed a wall which at times defied gravity by sticking rigidly to the very edges of steep drops. Our Munros for the day were Gharbh Chioch Mhor and Sgurr Na Ciche. These two fairly big mountains as it turned out proved to be quite easily done – due, I think, to our early starts and the height at which we began. From Sgurr Na Ciche we descended a long ridge onto Glen Dessary path. Soon we encountered two guys, Donald and Davy, working on a footbridge. They pointed out our route ahead. Descending to the head of Loch Nevis we eventually came to Sourlies bothy. We had intended to spend one night here but the bothy was occupied by a crowd from Maryhill in Glasgow, who were obviously high on drugs or drink and had the place trashed. We decided to camp near to the loch-side, as did Dennis, another walker who arrived just behind us; as it turned out he was a railway worker from Liverpool. Just along the shore from us there was another crowd camped, this time from Clydebank. They seemed to regard the place as their own private domain and were illegally hunting, shooting and fishing everything in sight. By now we were low on food and we had for our meal a couple of bits of cold bacon and mashed potatoes. That night I was to suffer severe stomach cramp, nausea and sickness, brought on, I suspect, by the people in the bothy contaminating the area around the water supply with human waste.

An early start around five-thirty saw us abandon camp, eaten alive by midges. Feeling awful, I struggled round the head of the loch and as the sun rose briefly over the mountains we had a meagre breakfast of more bacon and powdered potato at the new Carnoch bridge. Crossing this bridge was a significant moment for us: it marked our entry into Knoydart proper. By now the mist had come down as we battled on up Meall Buidhe. Navigating in mist, we followed the ridge round to a top marked as Druim Leac A' Shith, or as we named it 'The Drum of Leaking Shit' – ah well, that's the 'Glasgow Garlic' for you I suppose. By the time we reached the summit of Luinne Bheinn or 'Loony Bin' we were well knackered and were only too pleased to fall out onto the Mam Barrisdale path near its summit. I must have been feeling much better by now, and our spirits lifted as we set off down towards the village of Inverie, the main centre of habitation on the Knoydart peninsula. There we booked into the estate-run hostel. To our dismay we learned that the village store was closed, but the railwayman Dennis arrived soon after us and came to our rescue with some rolls. We were grateful for them to tide us over till the shop opened the following day.

This was not quite the end of the Knoydart walk. Next morning after a long lie-in we made pancake batter for breakfast then went for a walk into the village. As soon as the shop opened we bought a whole load of food and went back to the hostel and had a huge feast. During the day another walker arrived at the hostel – Harry, a lorry driver who came from Fauldhouse. He was obviously new to the hills and, as they say, he had a large opinion of himself. To get away from him, Rab, Dennis and myself spent a glorious afternoon sunning ourselves on the shore just in front of Inverie House. In the evening we decided to go to the only pub for miles around, the estate-owned Forge. Here we met Donald and Davy, whom we saw previously working on the bridge, and we proceeded to have a convivial evening. At some point Big Harry from Fauldhouse joined us and the evening wore on with plenty of swally. As we all walked back, a half bottle was passed back and forth among us.

Back at the hostel Big Harry by this time wanted to round off his evening with a good old-fashioned punch-up and decided to try and goad the young estate worker Davy into a toe-to-toe sparring bout. Dennis the Englishman, appalled by this barbaric Scots behaviour, had quickly disappeared upstairs to his bed. Meanwhile Rab, who was now well pissed, was swaying drunkenly between Mad Harry and the boy, trying to defuse the

Meeting the Garrygulloch cavalry
on the Mam Barrisdale path

situation, and he says, 'See a' youse big handsome bastards, yese ar a' the same: wan or two drinks an yese wannt tae hiv a go at sumbuddy hauf yer size.' Harry looked at Rab with a puzzled look. Not quite sure what to make of Rab swaying about in front of him, wondering if he was being flattered or, as we say in Glasgow, 'having the pish ripped from him'. I had visions of Harry going nuts and giving us all, especially Rab, a good doing, so we got Davy to leave and I shoved Rab up the steep stairs to his bed.

Have you ever tried to put a drunk to his bed? It's not an easy thing to do. They have an annoying habit of getting back up again. So I eventually put out the lights and tried to settle down but no sooner had I done so when I heard Rab get up again. Fuck it! Just where the bloody hell did the old fool think he was going? I was worried that he might take a header down the steep stairs and break his drunken neck, so I got back up and went after him. He had staggered right across the landing stark bollock naked and into the wee Englishman's bedroom, and there he was sitting on his bed telling him how much he liked him. Poor Dennis was sat bolt upright, with his blankets wrapped tightly around him, terrified at the sight of a naked Scotsman seemingly trying to get into his bed. Again I managed to get him back into his own bed. By this time Harry, who was in the same room as us, had crawled up the stairs and passed out on his own bunk. With them all in their own beds I again went back to mine. Not long after I again hears Rab up and blundering about the room in the dark, so 'Fuck it!' says I, 'If he falls down the stairs and breaks his sodding neck that's his problemo!' But after a few minutes I hears him stop and then the sound of him having a piss. Oh shit! Up I staggers and reach for the light switch, and there stands Rab with a stupid grin on his face freely pissing all over a comatose Harry. Horrified, I bundle him back into his bunk thinking, 'Harry's gonna fuckin kill us when he wakes up.' So very early next morning a rather bemused Rab is dragged out of bed, force-fed his breakfast and marched the half mile to the ferry slipway. I was praying that we would catch the ferry to Mallaig and be long gone before Harry woke up. This was not to be. Just as the painfully slow approaching ferry hove into sight, Big Harry walked onto the pier. I thought, 'Oh shit, this is it! We've come all this way just to die at the hands of a nutter!' Striding up, Harry commented on such a good night and that he remembered so little of what happened. In all of the years he had been drinking, he said that last night was the only time he had ever wet the bed, even managing to piss all over his rucksack and gear as well as the wall and bedside cabinet. Only when the ferry had reached Mallaig and we were safely on the train to Glasgow did I enlighten Rab as to why he had been dragged out that morning.

'We're jist travellers'

MYSELF, RAB DOYLE AND STUKKY Stirling set off on a fine bright day on 30 June. Rab and I had gone up to Glasgow early to collect a hired van. The trip almost ended before it began. The vehicle we were meant to have had been damaged and we were offered a Transit instead. This was bad news as a small van was much better suited for our purposes, so we stuck to our guns and eventually got the vehicle we wanted.

Picking up wee Stukky Stirling in Paisley and collecting all our gear we set off for the far north. Our route was up the A82 by Loch Lomond, stopping at Bridge of Orchy for a meal. We only stopped once more, at Invergarry for petrol, and pushed onwards till we reached our first campsite up a quiet Glen Glass to the east of Ben Wyvis. As we set up the tents – a two-man one for Rab and I and a one-man for Stukky – we were assailed by hordes of midges. Rab Doyle spent a fruitless time tying to inflate a lurid but cheap airbed that wee Stukky had purchased for 99p.

Day two, Sunday, we were up at five and broke camp quickly, pursued by the midge hordes. Driving to the end of the glen we set off up the hill at seven sharp. Our way took us through a large fenced-off area, home to a herd of red deer which we passed very warily. I have seen deer in a zoo try to attack through a fence and we were not taking any chances. Climbing up into the mist we pushed on along a continuous ridge with many tops. The mist would occasionally clear to give us brief glimpses of the sun. Once or twice we thought that we were lost, but we eventually made the top of Ben Wyvis.

A bearing from the cairn took us off along a long easy ridge but left us with some rough walking to where we had left the van. Back on the road again we drove via Lairg to near the Crask Inn where we turned off onto a side road and began to set up camp at the foot of our next hill, Klibreck. We were getting into a routine for setting up camp, with Rab on airbed pump and Stukky on

'Puffing Billy', with myself as chief tent erector.

Another early rise, six-thirty, and this time with few midges around we had brekky. Leaving the tents up we set off along the path leading to Klibreck. In cloud and rain we ascended a long ridge to our first top where the mist began to clear, letting us proceed around the ridge. On reaching the summit we sat about

Rab and Stukky on the summit of Kilbreck

while the mist cleared away giving us spectacular views of Sutherland and the hills to the north. The trig point on Klibreck is one of the few that I have seen to have been a target of many lightning strikes. We descended to the west side of the hill down to the road which gave us a bit of a road walk. But we were not unhappy about that; we were more disappointed that despite displaying signs advertising beer the Crask Inn was at that time a private house. Returning to camp we had our meal, broke camp and drove to the Altnaharra Inn where we did obtain beer. Wee Stukky even had a wash and nicked soap and toilet paper, 'A' guid stuff,' says he.

Refreshed, we drove the short distance to our next camp at the foot of Ben Hope, the most northerly Munro. As we were setting up camp a car drew up and who should lean out of the window but Hughie Hart of the Gleniffer. He had been 'fishing', probably on the Duchess of Westminster's estate. We knew, and he knew that we knew, he had a load of fish, but he wasn't for sharing anything with mere walkers. Once more up at six-thirty, we again left the tents and van to set off up the hill. Ploughing almost straight up and into the mist we reached the summit at nine-thirty. The very brief views to the north were of Ben Loyal. As we swung off the summit and along the long backbone of this hill the mist eventually cleared away to leave us in sunshine. The mountain is formed of long escarpments and we descended along these to come down on the road at a farm next to a large broch, pounding along another stretch of road back to camp. After a drum-up we packed up and drove on, passing through Durness, home of the Smoo Cave, and skirting Loch Eriboll, a place Stukky had visited while on convoy escort to Russia, when it was a safe haven used by wartime convoys. Turning south, we had to push hard to catch the ferry at Kylesku. Nowadays there is a fine bridge to speed you on your way.

Arriving at Inchnadamph on a stunning evening, we set up camp on the shore of Loch Assynt where Stukky cooked the evening meal – when I say 'cooked', what I mean is that he knelt on a little prayer-type mat cranking up his 'Puffing Billy' stove while Rab and I ran about handing food and plates, opening cans, peeling potatoes, and so on. Later we retired to the nearby hotel for beer. That night, back in the tent, I found it difficult to drop off to sleep with the noise of a nearby boat lying on the shore. The breeze was slapping the waves against its hull and making it crunch on the gravel beach. I could not figure out why it kept on – the tide must have to go out at some time. It was only the next morning that I realised that Loch Assynt is an inland loch.

With our customary early start we set off up the glen to climb Conival in swirling mists. Conival and Ben More Assynt are big rough hills of broken rocks. On the summit we met a young guy from Edinburgh – we had met him previously when we were at A'Chuil bothy in Knoydart. On our descent the mists cleared to give terrific views. Obviously we were missing the best weather of the days due to our early starts.

Breaking camp we had a leisurely drive to Ullapool where we went to the town campsite. The town was busy with eastern

Camping at Inchnadamph: the shores of Loch Assynt

European factory-fishing-ship crews. Many had not experienced western living. They had descended upon Ullapool and were systematically buying up all the consumer goods they could lay their hands on. We could see them loading up their ships' lifeboats with fridges, washing machines, televisions and anything else they could not obtain in their own countries. This provided a mini boom for the town. One day I saw that one of the lifeboats had a Lada car sat across the gunwales astride two planks.

We soon tired of watching their antics and headed off for a few beers at the Ceilidh Place, where a folk singer was playing. Rab, possessed with drink, eventually began to sing too. The resident singer, unable to match Rab's deep baritone voice, found himself accompanying Rab as he took over as the star turn. Returning to camp was difficult with us trying to negotiate a four-foot wall while drunk.

Next morning, which was supposed to be a rest day, found us itching to get going again. Around lunchtime we set off on a short drive to Inverlael, and at one o'clock we walked into the Dheargs. Climbing two Munros in good weather, we set up camp on the col at Beinn Dhearg. After cooking a meal we took a short walk along a wall which led to the summit. From there, about nine on a stunning evening, we had views of both Little Loch Broom and Loch Broom to the west and the rolling hills of the Fannich range to the east. On this walk we were not using the full tent but just the flysheet, with us all carrying tent pegs, poles and so on between us.

A very early start around four found us on Cona Meal by six. At one point we left the packs and bagged another peak after which we had a good drum-up. As the day wore on the weather turned to rain and we still had a long way to go to reach the furthest-away hill, Seana Braigh – we renamed it 'Shaun O'Brien',

Evening on the Dheargs

the Irishman's hill. After a long plod up and down lesser hills we reached the col onto Seana Braigh. Here we left the bags and chuntered up to the top in our shorts and waterproofs. The walk out was long and tedious and it was three weary wee men who drove back to Ullapool, grateful for a pint in the Argyll Hotel.

The following day we were too shattered to do anything other than wash ourselves and our gear and restock food supplies. Wee Stukky, his arse almost hanging out of badly torn breeches, had met a Dutch couple on the camping ground. They came from a port called Skaddam which Stukky had visited while in the navy. The woman stitched up his torn breeks and the husband gave him a good drink of Skaddam gin. Later, much refreshed, we found ourselves at a ceilidh at the Far Isle Hotel.

Back to early rising, we drove south, stopping to view the gorge at Corrieshalloch. As the day improved we drove to Kinlochewe where we set off to ascend the stunning hill of Slioch (The Spear). After nearly getting the start wrong we set off under a scorching hot sun and traversed around the summit tops of this fabulous mountain with its staggering views of the Fisherfield Forest and Loch Ewe. At one point on this quite complicated hill we met a guy with a wee kiddie with him. Late that afternoon, footsore and weary and well burnt by the sun, we decided to have a drink in the Loch Maree Hotel after coming back down off the hill.

The Loch Maree Hotel is quite a magnificent edifice, with a huge statue of Queen Victoria at the front and a vast car park full of Daimlers and Rolls-Royces. We were obviously not welcome – not surprising considering that after days in the hills we literally stank.

Trying to enter by the front door we were headed off by a rather large chap dressed in tweeds and deerstalker. He directed us round to the rear, down a long corridor and stairs which eventually led to a tiny room well behind a large, sumptuous lounge. This was where the gillies sat after a day's shooting or fishing, in this wee bare room while the laird or fat customer sent through a wee dram. The final insult was them serving us beer in silly little glasses: I don't think they knew what a pint tumbler looked like. So to hell with this, we made our exit straight through the main lounge chock full of toffs, and Rab was heard to bellow 'Victory tae the fucking miners', throwing them a clenched-fist salute. This was at the time of the miners' strikes of 1984. In an indignant cloud of dust we blasted off along the coast road passing Loch Ewe, Gairloch, Gruinard Bay, Loch Broom and by Dundonell in search of somewhere more appropriate for pilgrims like us.

We eventually made camp on the Desolation Road beside the old Fain bothy. The old ruin of Fain stands alone on the desolate moorland stretch of road that runs from Ullapool to Dundonell, from which there are distant views of An Teallach and Slioch. Although it is appropriate to describe the road as desolate it was in fact originally known as the Destitution Road. During the famine of 1847–8 it was constructed to provide employment for the local crofting population. The wild moor that it crosses was known as the Feighan. Before the road there was just a rough track, the route of the cattle drovers. Fain bothy then was the Feighan Inn and this was where the drovers, driving their herds of black cattle, stopped for food and shelter. On three separate occasions we camped beside Fain bothy. It may well be that we subconsciously felt it comforting camping there because it was – even if a ruin – a tangible sign of human habitation in such a wild and desolate place.

Early next morning we again set off into the hills. Wee Stukky gave two passing walkers a shout. They were obviously 'Chentlemen' walkers: they were wearing check shirts and ties. 'Haw, hey, see us! We're aff tae dae ra Fisherfield Six.' God knows what they thought looking at the three wee Glesga punters, especially the wee man with all his gear hanging in bits and pieces from his pack tied on with string.

We passed by Shenavall bothy in searing conditions. The heat was overpowering as we plodded up over Ben Chlabheimh and Sgurr Ban. It was so hot that the rocks were too warm to touch, and as we were about to ascend Sgor Ban we slavered with pleasure over a delicious can of pears. That night, dirty, exhausted and sunburned, we made camp just below the col of Sgurr Ban and Mullach Coire Mhic Fhearchair.

The heat was still oppressive and we knew what was coming: it was not long before a tremendous thunderstorm began, pounding rain drumming off our flysheet. Wrapped up in space blankets, Stukky and I were roasting due to our sunburn. As we lay there, there would be a blinding flash of light followed immediately by an almighty crash of thunder. The storm crashed and echoed all around us. At times there was no interval between the flash and bang: it must have been very close. I had visions of a lightning strike leaving three charred corpses wrapped in foil like a Colonel Saunders Kentucky Fried Chicken. At some point Rab went outside for a look-see and came back into the tent to inform us with his famous poker face, 'We'll huv tae move ra tent or get washed aff ra hill if yon wee lochan overflows!' At this, Stukky and I in chorus ceremoniously told Rab to fuck off; we were too cosy where we were. Finally it became apparent that we would have to do something and the sooner the better. Leaving Stukky with our packs and gear, Rab and I tried to lift the tent in one go. But this would not work, so we then had to dismantle and re-erect it in the dark, lit up at times by flashes of lightning, in a safer location, telling Stukky to 'Keep shouting! As long as we can hear ye . . .' Eventually the tent was sorted and we snuggled back in to fall into deep sleep. Dawn found the three of us all squashed to one side of the tent which was pitched at a crazy angle as well as being inside out. What did concern me was that we had re-sited the tent close to a sheer drop and that anyone going outside for a pee in the middle of the night would have had an unpleasant surprise as they fell off a cliff.

As we sat cooking our breakfast at the door of the tent we saw laid out before us a spectacular panorama of the Fannich hills. With an early start we soon found ourselves on our first summit of the day, Mullach Coire Mhic Fhearchair. Here we met a lone Englishman who said he had been in the RAF at the time of the Falklands War. When he left us we could hear him in the mist, roaring and bawling as he threw large rocks down into the corrie. The thunderstorm of the previous night must have set him off.

As the mist blew away to a fair day we progressed on to our next mountain, Bein Tarsuinn, with its flat summit. From here we had spectacular views of the serrated peaks of An Teallach (which we did not climb till later, on 20 October 1985, rather late in the year for us to travel so far to claim a hill – it had to be done because Billy Billings had gone on and on about how he had climbed 'An Chalack', as he called it, over forty years earlier). We camped along the road from the Dundonnell Hotel and as the nights were drawing in we made the mistake of spending the night in the bar. This was fatal. Others there with the same idea were also partaking in Dutch courage before tackling this fearsome hill. I had been drinking, for the first and only time, black rum and peppermint. The next morning Rab dragged me from the tent and forced me to eat a plate of greasy mince which I promptly spewed all over the road. Of the climb I remember little except crawling along on all fours looking into the corrie far below. I also recollect that the sky was pink and the hills were a deep red. I never drank and climbed again.

On the bealach between Tarsuinn and our next hill, A' Mhaighean, we stopped for a good drum-up before pushing onwards over A'Mhaighean, from which we had spectacular views all round the Fisherfield and beyond – especially along Loch Maree. Fortunately the hotel was not in sight. After another drum-up of tea we looked up at Ruadh Stac Mhor wondering what was the best way up. 'Ach, jist go straight up it,' says Stukky, and we did. It was the best way, for in no time at all we were sitting on the cairn, a well-built one of cemented rocks, not the usual trig point. As the day wore on we had a rough descent made worse by the blistering heat, more so as we reached the glen itself which was like a frying pan. After wading two rivers which were unusually low we reached Shenavall bothy. By this time I had had enough; my feet were on fire, I was suffering from sunburn and I was too exhausted to walk out that night.

However, unbeknown to Rab and me, a friend of Stukky's had stupidly said to the wee man that Fisherfield would be too much for him. This was like a red rag to a bull. Stukky was determined to prove him wrong and nothing was stopping him from walking out that night. Raging, I was forced to do so too. I realise now that it was anger that got me out. As we prepared to move off,

Stukky, who had been stuffing his face with cream crackers, grabbed a large American girl to give her a kiss on the cheek and left her covered in crumbs. In fact, we broke the normal record for doing the Fisherfield Four. What most people take four days to do, we did in just over thirty hours.

When we arrived back out at the road very late at night we drove along to the Dundonell Hotel, just in time for a quick pint. I angrily asked Stukky, 'Right, then! Whit dae we dae noo?' Of course Stukky pipes up, 'Och, ah ken a hostel we can go tae any time, day or night.' This was in the village of Achnasheen, according to him. This was ludicrous. It involved a long drive south; but off we drove into the night.

In the wee small hours and lit by a silvery moon we slowly entered the village. As I parked the van, Rab and Stukky were out with their sleeping bags and away round the back of a low building. As I followed I could hear the tactless wee bugger, 'Aye, this is the place a' right, jist see the rucksacks hingin oan ra wa.' At this, from the depths of the building emerged a large black dog barking its bloody head off! On hearing the dog I stopped in my tracks just as a figure emerged. I could see the moonlight shining on his bald head and what looked like a long red beard. He was wearing an Oor Wullie Winkie night-gown. But what really caught my attention were the barrels of a shotgun shining in the moon's light. An angry voice roared, 'Who the bloody hell are you?', at which the wee man pipes up, 'Oh, we're jist travellers.' This of course was the wrong reply.

'Travellers? Tinkers, bloody tinkers!' he shouts, and up comes the glinting gun barrel. 'Out, out, out!'

At this Rab gets a word in quickly. 'We're just climbers looking for the hostel.'

'Ye'r in the wrong bloody village. The hostel you want is ten miles up the bloody road!'

By this time I was back out at the van unable to stand up for laughing. Not only had we got the village wrong, we nearly had our heads blown off for entering someone's house and been mistaken for tinkers. With tails between our legs we quietly made it to the right place and found bunks for what remained of the night.

We lay till ten next morning and had a late breakfast. Needing a rest, we decided to go for a run in the van, so off we drove, west to Lochcarron, stopping for petrol. We passed the huge derelict oil platform building yards at Kishorn, now eerily deserted. Our route took us over the famous Bealach Nam Bo to the Applecross peninsula. Arriving at Applecross we went into the hotel for a pint. Driving on up the new road, only opened for about five years at that time, we saw a strange line of ruined houses near to the shore. Turning off for a closer look we found ourselves at a deserted village that looked strangely familiar. This was Lonbain, the location, as we later discovered, of a television film about life on the island of St Kilda. In the village we came to a 'black hoose'; there was smoke coming from it and flowers growing on the thatch roof. It was in fact inhabited by an old man called Duncan MacKenzie.

Duncan MacKenzie's black hoose

He wore an old fore and aft deerstalker hat with no aft and cut away round his large ears, making it look like a schoolboy's cap. Despite the isolation of the place he knew more about world events than we did, who had been in the hills for days. It seemed that he possessed a good radio. As he and wee Stukky got talking it transpired that Stukky knew him over fifty years before, when Duncan ran the nearby youth hostel for a brief time. After dinner we had a quiet night around the fire in the dark with a German family.

Next morning we drove a short distance along the road to Achnashellach Station where we parked the van and set off in rain

On the way back to the hostel, exhausted

and mist to our next three Munros. This was a long, tough day on big, hard hills, having to navigate on the tops by dead reckoning. We managed to complete the first two hills, Sgurr Ruadh and Beinn Liath Mhor. When we descended from these we were faced with a long trek in mist to our third mountain. This was Maol Chinn Dhearg.

Taking a direct compass bearing we went straight for the hill. Luck must have been with us that day: the bearing took us straight to a large gully which split the hill and ran right to its summit. However, as we climbed into mist so thick we could hardly see one another, the going became very steep till at one point the others were not so much in front of me but more above. Rab was actually pushing the wee man up the hill and at times I had to jump from side to side in the gully below as Stukky dislodged large rocks which kept flying past me in the mist. Eventually we reached the top where a large iron cross marked the summit. Our route off was down a long undulating slope which led us down the Fionn Glen. At one stage we had to stop for a rest and I clearly remember Rab having to spoon-feed Stukky a tin of sardines and make sure he chewed each bite. The wee man looked just like a wee stukky starling being fed worms.

At this point we were all very tired and were grateful to reach the path in the glen. Here we came upon an old building which turned out to be Fionn bothy. The bothy at that time was in quite good condition with furniture and fittings. Upstairs there were rooms, and the whole place was well lined with wood panelling. Moving on, we passed a huge white stone supposedly where a legendary Fingalian character tied his hound.

Eventually we found ourselves out on the road with a long hike back to the van. We tried to hitch a lift but there was so little traffic that we soon became resigned to a long weary haul back to the hostel. We even resorted to getting Stukky to limp even harder and when a small saloon car came along Rab tried flagging it down by jumping out in front of it, waving his arms around. The sight of Rab with a sunburnt face looking like a burst tomato only succeeded in frightening the terrified day-tripper.

This was a long, weary stagger in eventual darkness with us all strung out along the road, marching in silence, and by the time we got back to the hostel we were almost too tired to eat anything. Which was just as well, as the owner was sitting meditating in the dark and would not let us put lights on.

On a later visit to the area when I saw what we had climbed in mist I could only reflect on just how lucky we were to strike the route up the mountain that we did. A few yards on either side and we were dead men that day. We took two more days to drive home because we were so tired. We spent a night at Nancy Smith's hostel at Fersit and then home. In sixteen days we had conquered the most northerly Munros, twenty-one of them plus four tops, we had camped at the tops of mountains, bagged whole groups in one go, and nearly got our head blown off for our troubles.

The man whose house we had entered actually came along to the hostel to apologise for not giving us a cup of tea.

Glen Affric

UP IN THE NORTH-WEST ON the road to Skye lies the wild Glen Affric or, as we called it, Affaric. A glen with Munros for those who care to toil for their mountains the hard way. This was a short but memorable outing, the first in my wee red vw Jetta. For the first time we had independent transport. We were mobile, free to target the hills on our own. With a new set of wheels we could take the hills by storm. On this trip, we climbed over Ben Attow to spend a night in Altbeithe youth hostel in Glen Affaric. From the hostel we had a tremendous day on three of the Affaric hills. The most spectacular part was the walk out early on a stunning morning through the 'Gates of Affaric'. There was no rhyme or reason at that particular time to go into Glen Affric, but there are times when a name can capture the imagination. Who were we to resist the call to a place with a name like the Gates of Affric? My memory of the climb up Ben Attow, like many of the Munros, has long since vanished in a sea of pain. I only recall the long ridge to the summit and the circular trig point. However, the recollection of the summits from Ben Attow that day is a different matter: it was a day of sharp visibility and we could see forever, with many of our mountains marching off into the far distance. The top of Attow is a long whaleback which we traversed from end to end, and it was two sunburnt, weary, but happy wee men who staggered into the youth hostel that night.

At that time Altbeithe hostel was fairly well equipped and there was little evidence of vandalism. There were plenty of chairs and tables and a lot of homely touches such as drawings and sketches of the area. That night we had the place to ourselves – or so we thought. But late on a huge guy on his own appeared. He was from Newcastle or the Tyneside area and by the odd shape of his head and shoulders we immediately christened him 'the Sauce Boattle'. It seemed that he had been wandering about the area for about a week. He obviously had little or no food and we thought that he was looking to us to feed him. Having had to carry our own loads we were sharing with naebody.

Next morning Rab and I were up and away early. Our hills were to the north of the hostel and our climb started almost immediately. The reason we left early was that the Sauce Boattle had hinted he would tag along with us. The outlook weather-wise was for another even hotter day and this it proved to be. From the summits, visibility was hazy due to the blistering heat once the sun got up. Our route for the day took us out to outlying tops and back, and at one point both of us were wearing our waterproofs and little else in an attempt to keep the sun off us. At one summit, as we sat drinking in the view and trying to cool off, a runner appeared from nowhere in running shoes, shorts and tee-shirt: all he carried was a bottle of water in his hand. We never did see the Sauce Boattle again – he must have just moved on. With another bag of new Munros under the belt we returned to the hostel to find a couple of walkers who had just walked in that day. One of them was an old-timer who had only twelve Munros to do. He said to us that 'Each one should have a fell to oneself' – a strange sentiment, I thought. Who would want to own just one mountain? Although the hostel was quiet and we had a quiet evening and a good night's sleep, the glen around the hostel was busy enough with people camping. As they were doing some 'Chooky Embra' scheme they were not allowed to use the hostel. Hoping for, or rather dreading, the prospect of another hot day, we arose very early, around four o'clock in fact. In Scotland we never say out loud that we really hate walking on hot sunny days. But our walk out to the car along the glen would be like being in a frying pan. So there we were, up and away, looking along the glen with the mist beginning to rise from the hollows and folds in the ground. The sun was already high but our way was still in the shade of the nearby mountains. This would not last long and we pressed on towards our last obstacle, the Gates of Affric, now in front of us. We made it through just as the sun began to beat down upon us, but our way now was an easy downhill walk to Dornie where the car was parked.

The Gates were a turning point for us. From now on we began to tackle the Munros in earnest. We thought that summer would be a good one for weather, but it turned out that this was the best weekend's worth we were to get on the hills that year. But this did not deter us from big days in the big glens such as Strathfarrar and Mullardoch, and much more. Mullardoch was one of the few outings when wee Jimmy came with us. We sometimes felt that

Glen Affric youth hostel

we were doing bigger days than he would have liked. After a long hard day, on coming off the last of the Mullardoch hills, we sheltered beside a little building which was occupied by a young couple on honeymoon. They were waiting for a boatman to ferry them to the other end of the loch and were kind enough to let us brew up on the porch out of the rain. There was a chance, they said, that we could all get a sail out when the boat came and save a gruelling five-mile slog along the raised shore of the loch.

When the boatman, a huge teuchter, finally appeared, wee Jimmy enquired about a lift. With undisguised smugness the big teuchter boomed out, 'Och aye! That will chust be the fifteen pounds per head.' Before he had even finished Rab and myself were marching off along the shore. Nae big smug heilan' rascal was having that amount of money from us. As we left the scene we could hear the plaintive cry from Jimmy, 'Och, but we're the unemployed.' At least we had our pride. And anyway the walk had to be finished on foot or the map would never have looked right. Later, after a hard few miles walking along a pathless shore made difficult by the steepness of the hill as it ran into the loch, we reached the road at the end of the loch. About a hundred yards to the finish I had stopped to dig out a crust from the heel of an old white loaf – I was light-headed through hunger. Of course this was a daft thing to do – I had not enough spit to chew the damned thing and it was because I was messing around doing this that I missed what was, according to Rab, the highlight of the walk. It was the sight of the legendary Jimmy sinking to his knees and sighing in a very weak whisper, 'Oooh, that wis a big day.' We had managed to walk a legend into the ground and I was too busy chewing on a crust of bread.

'Is this ra effing bothy?'

TARF BOTHY LIES JUST TO the north of Glen Tilt. This was a two-day outing, Rab and I with the Gleniffer boys, to bag four Munros in the area known as the Ring of Tarf, with a bothy night in the 'Tarf Hotel'. As usual, and despite pre-arranged plans, we ended up travelling independently of the boys. They went up north the previous night while we drove up in the morning. We walked up Glen Tilt from the Old Bridge of Tilt while the boys walked in the opposite direction and spent the night in Allt Sheicheachan bothy. We had a pleasant, easy walk up the Tilt and at one point we messed around on a bucket bridge before climbing our Munro for the day, Ben a Chalmain. This we did by climbing up the long ridge on the east side of the Allt Craonidh and then a left turn onto the summit of Chalmain. From here we had an easy descent over Meall Tionail to the Tarf bothy.

In its day the building must have been very well appointed. There was an 'AA Approved' sign on the door. At one end was what we took to be a sort of boiler room, with pipes running all around the walls. Alas, when we got there the only habitable part was a small room in the centre of the building. It was still wood-panelled and had a fireplace, a few chairs, a table and three beds with no mattresses, but sprung with concave springs. There was a table made from a door. We could tell it was a door because it still had the doorknob on it as well as the keyhole and a key sticking out of the lock. Someone had drawn sketches of themselves and had stuck them on the walls; unimpressed by the unknown artist's talents we later used these self-portraits to light the fire.

The plan was for the boys to do the hills in the opposite direction from us and for us all to rendezvous at the Tarf bothy, spend one night there and set off again the next day in opposite directions. So while we had an easy first day they had a long, hard one. To make things comfortable we found a spade and a supply of dried peat and soon had a huge fire going with bogwood and peat. Much later in the evening, which had turned wet and misty, we could see the lads approaching in the distance. They were pretty wet and weary but they still had to wade across the Tarf Water. When they clumped into the cosy, warm bothy our welcoming was deflated by dripping-wet wee Jimmy exclaiming, 'Is ris ra fuckin bothy?' There is no pleasing some folk. That night we had a cosy bothy night with the Paisley men, Big Al, Stukky Alexander, Wee Stukky Stirling, Jimmy Gallacher and Andy Murdoch, and us all chattering away good style. Typically, they cooked individual meals for themselves, with the sound of five different smelly primus stoves spluttering away. Settling down for the night there were two to a bed sleeping head to toe. Stukky and Andy for some reason had made their beds up on the table. I don't know why – the floor was just as hard and you couldn't fall off. However there they were and of course Stukky finds that he is lying with the doorknob and key stuck in his back and wriggles around trying to get comfortable. Finally Andy roars in exasperation, 'Dae ye hae the poseetion?'

Early next morning it was Rab and I who had a big day before, and the others had a lie-in. We were up at four and away by five. In rain and thick mist we crossed the Tarf Water and made our way slowly up onto Sron Na Macranaich, then up onto the grassy south ridge of An Sgarsoch to its summit. From here it was a drop onto the col at about 700 or so metres, then north-west up to the summit of Carn An Fhidleir. It was here on these flattish grassy tops that horse and cattle fairs are supposed to have taken place long ago. Today it seems too remote, but at some time in the past many of these deserted glens had much more life in them, so who knows? As we left this top the day began to improve. After all, it was still quite early. We began to make a wide sweep to the west then south, following most of the high ground and heading for our last Munro of the trip, Beinn Dearg. We did not realise it at the time but we also walked over a solitary Corbett, Beinn Bhreac, at 912 metres almost a Munro. Standing almost twelve kilometres north of Blair Atholl, Beinn Dearg is a sharp peak of red granite with large scree slopes over which we toiled to the trig point. Our early start meant that we were now coming off our hills at the warmest part of the day. Our way off Beinn Dearg down the south ridge led us into a deep corrie where we came onto a stalkers' track leading down the Allt Sheicheachan burn to the bothy. This was where the boys had spent their first night, and while there, they were wakened during the night by police who

Inside Tarf bothy

were looking for two women missing in the hills. As the coppers shouted up, 'Is there ony weemin there?', they received the reply, 'Naw, bit if ye fin ony wull ye send em up?'

The bothy was very clean and tidy. What struck me as unusual was the floor, which was flagged with concrete slabs. It was nice to be inside for a while out of the heat of the day, but we had no plans to spend a night here so we were all too soon back on the road again. As we walked on, the track met up with another in Glen Banvie that runs through to Glen Bruar and enters the extensive forestry plantation surrounding the Blair Castle estates. From here on it was only a short distance back to the Old Bridge of Tilt where we had parked the car.

A Pint Called Alice

CONFIDENT THAT WE COULD repeat the success of our previous northern expedition the year before, when we had hammered most of the most northerly Munros in one week, we collected Stukky and drove north in the wee Jetta up the A9. We stopped only at the transport cafe in Dalwhinnie for a truck driver's breakfast and later at Muir of Ord for petrol, pushing on over the new Kessock bridge at Inverness and west to Aultguish Inn, where we called in for beer. That night we put up the tent at Fain bothy on Destitution Road, a campsite from previous trips. Here we met up with John Cameron of the HF, who had decided to join us. The next day saw us as usual up and away to an early start. This time we used two cars to give us transport at the walk's end. On a long, fine, sunny day we traversed the whole range of mountains known as the Fannichs. We set off from a wide sweeping bend on the Destitution Road towards Loch a' Bhraoin, and a long slog up the ridge of Drum Reidh took us onto the main ridge where a right turn brought us to the first peak of A'Chailleach. The rest of the day saw us weave in and out along the tops of Sgurr Breac, Sgurr nan Each, which looks down into Loch Fannich, and then on to Sgurr nan Clach Geala, the highest of the group. So it went on – each way we turned there were mountains galore: the Deargs to the north, An Teallach to the west and Wyvis to the east. We trekked to the most easterly of the group, then about-turned and re-climbed one top and Meall Gorm before dropping down from Creachain Rairigdh to the Loch an Fhuar-thuill Mhoir, where we would camp for the night high among the hills. While we drummed up tea that night, Stukky, the eternal scrounger, who as usual contributed little in the way of food or cooking, had gone over to John Cameron's tent, giving us the impression that he was sharing Cameron's food . Well, with tea and a Dixie full of food and the food on his face, I assumed that was what he was doing. So Rab and I took what little we had left and split it two ways.

Just then the wee man reappeared, looking for his share of our meal. We ended up with one quarter of the food while Stukky had half of it plus what John had given him. That night Rab and I went to bed hungry and angry.

Next morning, an early start saw us break camp and quickly climb the last Munro of Beinn Liath Mhor Fannich with an easy walk out to the road at Loch Glascarnoch. As Cameron left us here and went charging away to meet other Munro-baggers in the Glen Sheil area, we celebrated our climb with a Highland fling at the roadside before we drove to the nearby Aultguish Inn to camp below the huge dam. A bar meal and a few pints of a local brew called Alice – which looked like lager rather than an ale and was so easy to drink – rounded off a great day. It was while waiting for our meal that Stukky sat beside other walkers already eating their meal, almost slavering at the mouth till one of them gave in and asked if he wanted a chip. Stukky immediately grabbed it off the plate, saying, 'Aye, jist tae taste wan.' We just cringed with embarrassment, unable to control the wee man. Early next morning, well hung over, we were wakened by Stukky wanting to get into the car so that he could wash. Lying in a tent with the sun streaming through its walls and with someone inside your head pounding away with a steam hammer is not a nice feeling. Trying to open your eyes is painful enough, but trying to raise yourself to an upright position only starts your head and body spinning uncontrollably – and defying the impulse to lie down can induce involuntary vomiting.

Well, Stukky – who was not in the same condition and is well known for unnecessary early rising – persisted in his desire to get his shaving gear from the car and look for water to wash in. Even in my befuddled condition I realised that we were camped below a huge hydro dam, behind which were millions of gallons of water – and that if I could rise I would fuckin' throw him in the bloody thing. For a while he disappeared and I drifted off into a comatose state. Until suddenly he appeared in the tent, brandishing two steaming hot tin cups of tea which were thrust into our hands, inflicting burns and spilling hot liquid over our sleeping bags. This was probably the worst start to a day, and never since have I seen or wished to see another pint of Alice.

When we eventually broke camp we drove south and then west to Achnasheen. Here we parked the car in the village and set off for to climb Fionn Beinn. This was a fairly short day with an almost straight-up-and-down approach and descent. The only problem for the day was the weather, dull and misty on the tops with showers. As we sat at the summit cairn, wee Stukky pulled three half-rotten apples from the bottom of his pack and passed them around.

The hydro dam

They must have been there quite some time and were so bruised and mushy that the minute the wee man turned his back both of us simultaneously threw them as far over the cliffs as we could. When we came back down we drove the ten miles along the road to Gerry's hostel at Craig.

When we arrived at Gerry's that night we met a rather loud English 'chap' who rather got up everyone's nose with his bragging about his exploits. For once we were pleased to have Stukky with us, because every place the Englishman mentioned wee Stukky had been there too, whether it was the Alps, the Himalayas, Australia's Northern Territories or New Zealand's Milford Trail. That night Stukky put yon bloke's gas at a very small peep. There was also an affable young guy called Mike Stott. He came from Banff and had been wandering around the hills for a week or so on his own, mostly half drunk. He had just been on Skye and by his description it seemed he had gone up and down the Inaccessible Pinnacle the wrong way round. There was also a German pair, Johan and Reinhart.

By this stage of the trip, wee Stukky's behaviour had become increasingly difficult. I'm not sure if it was because we were all quite weary or if, as often happens as a group, we were suffering from 'cabin fever'. Being stuck in a tent for a time in bad weather can make even the best of friends fall out.

An early start the next morning saw us with only a short drive across the railway to park up a forest track. This would prove to be a long day of mist and rain. As we walked clear of the trees we were soon below 910-metre Sgurr nan Ceannaichean . The road took us quickly into the glen Pollan Bhuide. From here we turned and climbed straight up onto the hillside. It was not long before we were in the mist and having to navigate our way. On a lousy day of cold, driving rain and mist we struggled round the three Munros of Sgurr nan Ceannaichean, Moruisg and Maol Lunndaidh, and the top of Carn nam Fiaclan. We fought our way along towards the summit to Moruisg. I was in front following a line of cairns leading to the summit, when behind me Rab and Stukky (whom Rab was helping along) were surprised to see the Englishman from Gerry's appear from a right angle to the ridge. They saw him kick the marker cairn, declare it the summit and, before they could enlighten him about his mistake, disappear straight off the ridge in the opposite direction. I was disappointed not to see him again – it would have been nice to inform him that he did not touch the summit at all.

From Moruisg we had a descent to the valley floor, to the ruin of an old lodge where we were grateful to take shelter before tackling the other hills that day. The awful weather sapped us all. At one stage we had become so badly disorientated in the mist that we were descending the hill in the wrong direction – it was only when we sighted a loch below us that we realised our mistake and could pinpoint our exact location. It meant having to re-climb a steep hill we had only just come off. It was only because wee Stukky was in too exhausted a state to argue with us that we found it comparatively easy to convince him that we were indeed climbing a different hill altogether.

It was a very tired trio of wee men that got back to the hostel that night, too exhausted to cook much and quite happy to sit in the dark and meditate with 'mine host'. The next day Stukky was too tired. We were relieved when he decided not to climb and instead opted to go for a walk with the young guy from Banff. So off went Rab and me on another foul day to return to the same glen and this time turn up on the path to the Bealach Bernais. Battered and blasted by the elements we clawed our way over the two Munros of Sgurr A'Chaorachain and Sgurr Choinnich. At one stage I could hear Rab shouting on me but I just clung on to rocks, too battered and soaked to answer. When we did top the last cairn we sat in the lee of some rocks and snatched a hot drink. This is when Rab pulled his classic begging face and tried to persuade me that the ridge leading off into the mist was only about half a mile at the most and it was a top we might never get back to. I put up little struggle, of course: I knew we had to go on. And so we did, and it was just as well – as we got to the cairn the mist parted for the first time that dismal day and gave us views of a wild, empty wilderness, one we would never see again.

Later that night, when Rab and I returned to the hostel, we found that Gerry had gone off to the pub and left Stukky in sole charge of the place. He had obviously let this position of power go straight to his head, otherwise he might just have had the sense to prepare a hot meal for us after such a wild day. I must have made some comment to this effect for he immediately went for me in one of his classic blowups. As he ranted at me I was too tired to take him seriously and started laughing at him, just as a huge notice-board on the wall fell onto the floor with an almighty crash, whereupon he stumped off in a huff. It got worse. Later, the lad from Banff came into the room and proceeded to cut his toe-nails with scissors at the same time as eating a cold pie and guzzling a can of coke, belching loudly. The wee man cracked up at the bemused guy and started slagging him off for his unhealthy eating habits. Stukky retired to bed early that night but at the crack of dawn there he was, rustling polythene bags to make sure we were wakened early. I suppose we should have been grateful that at least no hot tin cups of scalding tea were thrust at us. By now we had had enough and made up our minds that we were going home. A week of cabin fever with the wee man had been too much of a strain. Still, we had climbed fifteen Munros and six tops in a week of rotten weather.

The Old Kilpatrick Hills

FROM THE BEGINNING OF 1986 till recently, old Rab and I spent many days walking on the Old Kilpatrick hills. These low, rolling hills have time and again proved their worth in keeping us fit enough to tackle many of our big outings without having to travel far, especially in the winter months. At times Rab had to be cajoled into walking them, but when he had finished the Munros he grudgingly began to appreciate them for what they are worth. On many bitterly cold winter days – and even nights – we dragged ourselves to the summit of Duncolm at a height of about 411 metres. We saw many different birds – grouse, duck, grebe, curlew, meadow pipit, spotted woodpecker, green woodpecker, heron, goosander, wheatear, wren, buzzard, red-throated diver. On spring days our spirits would soar listening to the skylark sing. On other occasions we saw otters, hares, stoats, foxes, roe deer. Once when we were approaching the trig point on Duncolm we were surprised to see a grey squirrel sat on the top, preening himself in the warm sun. As we quietly surrounded the trig to see his reaction he looked over his shoulder at me then ran down the side and straight towards me. He ran between my legs and, before I could react, up the back of my legs, digging his sharp claws into my skin. As I jumped about in surprise he leaped up onto my rucksack then jumped to the ground and made off into the heather.

Our route usually took us up an escarpment covered with an old natural wood which, due to sheep, is unlikely to regenerate. This route is on good man-made paths and looks across the Clyde to the Erskine hospital – once the residence of Lord Blantyre of Erskine who owned these Kilpatrick hills – to our first trig point called the Slacks. From here we can view the whole of Glasgow and the Clyde valley. To the south immediately below is the village of Old Kilpatrick and the Erskine Bridge (built in 1972), and way beyond can be seen the Border hills and the Ayrshire coast with the mass of Ailsa Craig – known as Paddy's Milestone. Beyond the Renfrew hills of Misty Law we can see the peaks on the Isle of Arran. Westwards lies the tail o' the bank at Greenock with the Cowal hills beyond. To the north the vista ranges from the Arrochar mountains to Loch Lomond and Ben Lomond. North from the summit of the Slacks we can see the volcanic plug that forms Duncolm's round top. The middle distance shows the

Glasgow and the Clyde Valley
from Humphreys Road

best side of the Campsie hills, with Earl's Seat the highest point and in the distance the Meikle Bin. Beyond the Campsies, the mountains of Perthshire are just a mass of peaks. Just beyond Duncolm you can clearly see the rolling shapes formed by the cooling lava where lies the well-known rock formation the Whangie.

The Whangie was where we trained with the Gleniffer boys in the use of ropes and abseiling before we made our assault on the Cuillins of Skye. Although tame hills compared with some we had wandered among, the OKs caught us out more than once. On one occasion we managed to become completely lost three times in the one day. Another time saw us experience a long, tough day made difficult by having no food or drink and stumbling off in complete darkness. On one solo training run, travelling light and carrying nothing, I got caught out near the top of Duncolm in a thunderstorm. Out in open country with thunder crashing out almost directly overhead is an unpleasant experience. With each crash I threw my walking pole away and myself flat on the ground. Torrential rain came on, quickly turning to three-quarters-of-an-inch hailstones which hammered painfully on my unprotected head and shoulders. This lasted for what seemed like a very long time, till the thunder moved on over towards the distant Campsie hills.

On some days, especially in winter with a dusting of snow, you can make out on the slopes near the Slacks the shapes of bomb craters, a reminder of the Clydebank Blitz. Whether the pilots of the Luftwaffe simply dumped their bomb load or were deceived by dummy lights in these hills is cause for speculation. Near one crater where the heather had been burned I once found a large bomb fragment weighing some forty pounds.

Hostels, Bothies, Howffs and Tents

AS WE BEGAN TO GO TO THE hills in earnest it soon became apparent that many were just too far away to reach in a day's travel, especially on our early trips when we were limited to using public transport. Weather and the time of the year had to be taken into consideration – after all, winter days were short. Accommodation had to be sought, and for this we turned to the Scottish youth hostels. We made much use of them in the early years. The hostels in those days were an adventure in themselves. Historically, they were instrumental in promoting outdoor pursuits such as cycling and hiking for many in the early days of the outdoor revolution. I still remember my father and relations talking about using them before, and especially during, the war, when the roads were very quiet. In these days it was normal for hikers to walk from the city to some of the nearer hostels. Unlike those earlier hostellers, we had the whole weekend off work to go to our hills, although when I first started, a Saturday morning was part of the working week.

Over the last thirty years that I have used the hostels much has changed. Hostelling is much less spartan – upgraded facilities now cater more for the foreign backpacking tourist doing Scotland in a week or two on a well-worn tourist trail. The ideals that the hostels began with have largely been abandoned in that their purpose was to provide inexpensive accommodation to young people and others of limited means. However, we cannot really complain at what they have become as many Scots turned their backs on our hostels, preferring to seek warmer climes for holidays.

Favourite hostels for us were the small ones with little or no facilities, often remote and difficult to reach. The wardens themselves were a broad mix of personalities. We never really came across many of the well-known characters who ran them, such as Dom Capaldi of Ratagan. The wardens we met all seemed to be out-and-out nutcases or cranks. Whether they came that way or whether it was the job that drove them nuts, I was never quite sure. I suppose constantly handing out chores did that to them. It also seemed odd to me that many wardens were non-Scots. I

Ben Alder bothy

remember booking into Glen Nevis and the warden expressing relief to meet a fellow Scot for the first time in weeks.

Whenever we used the hostels, whether in small or large groups, we kept pretty much to ourselves and got on with the business of going to the hills. But if wee Stukky or Billy Billings was with us there was always bound to be a show. Stukky and Billy just loved to be the centre of attraction wherever they went. On one occasion Rab and Bill had been on Ben Nevis in unusually hot weather, so hot, in fact, that a Frenchman had died that day on the hill from dehydration and heatstroke. After booking into the hostel, Rab and Billy went for a pint in a nearby bar. Much later, when they returned, Rab grabbed hold of Billy and in no uncertain terms warned him that he was to go straight into the dormitory, not to turn lights on and quietly to go straight to his bunk. Billy shot Rab an insolent don't-dare-meddle-wi'-me look but nodded in the affirmative. Of course, the minute Bill gets in the dorm the first thing he does is switch on the lights. This produces an immediate chorus of groans from the other occupants vainly trying to sleep in the stifling heat. Many were lying with sunburnt arms and legs sticking out of their bunks. Billy, ignoring Rab's angry but futile signals to behave, defiantly sticks out his jaw and swings his head from side to side, then heads straight for the windows, tripping over outstretched arms and legs, and proceeds to close all the windows in the dormitory – noisily. Now that he has wakened half the place he clatters around getting washed, shaved and changed. When finally the whole dorm is wide awake he swings himself up between two bunks and starts using them as parallel bars – and gets into his pre-bedtime workout routine. The push-ups, sit-ups and the whole routine – a throwback to the thirties health-culture movement – went on for about twenty minutes. When this is over at last, he begins to smear his limbs with Olbas (or, as we called it, 'Ould Bass'), a foul-smelling lotion straight from a football changing room that immediately has everyone's eyes streaming with tears. With a final flourish he switches off the light and gets into bed. No wonder Rab came near to strangling the wee man.

On a weekend at Ratagan hostel, as we left to head off to climb Sgritheall, I turned to Rab and told him that I had put his boots in the boot of the car. 'Aw naw ye didnae,' he replied, with his usual

Ryovan the Red bothy

poker face. 'Naw, ah'm werrin them.' I had lifted someone else's boots by mistake. We were by now well down the road heading for our hill. We debated what to do and decided that the best thing was to go climb our hill and drop off the boots at the hostel on the way back. This we did – after all, the hills came first. Later that day I took the boots into the hostel to hand in to the warden. He told me that they belonged to a huge Englishman who was furious, thinking his boots had been nicked, and had gone off to nearby Kyle of Lochalsh to purchase a new pair. With this news I left them and made a rapid exit.

In summer the hostels were warm and stuffy, with windows often shut to keep out the midges. In winter they were freezing, grim places, warm enough in the kitchen or common room but miserable in the cold dormitories. Late one winter's night we arrived at Killin hostel cold, wet and hungry. We had to hammer on the doors and windows to gain entry and when the warden did open up it was obvious he wasn't too pleased to be bothered with us; this despite the fact that the hostel season was still on.

Not all hostels were near the hills we intended to climb. This meant using other means. Bothies were mostly open buildings, some maintained by the Mountain Bothies Association, others by estates. The bothies enabled us to reach some of the more remote and isolated mountains. They could be anything from a crude three-sided shelter to a substantial one-storey building. The bothies were a necessary means of shelter which we were happy to make use of, but in hindsight they were dirty and often vandalised hovels.

On our first visit to Shenevall bothy we found a place that had been well used over the years by countless climbers and walkers. Like many others it was very basic and dirty but in recent years, with nearly everybody's granny doing the Munros, I would not be surprised to see curtains and carpets in there. Corryhully was just a dirt floor with a broken fireplace and a roof so full of holes that you could lie in your sleeping bag and view the stars through them. I have since heard that the roof has been replaced and electric lighting installed.

The highlight of any bothy night was the bothy fire. Rab and I for some reason were lucky to have spent many merry nights around such legendary fires. The fire was a focal point around which wet socks and clothing vied for space. Once everyone had eaten, often bottles of holy watter or whisky and such like were produced. Arguments would blow up over religion, football, politics, in fact anything to start a rammy. Being far away from law and order, heated discussions would be taken outside to be settled with a square go – a primitive form of square-dancing mixed with violence. Calls of nature took these bothy bums outside, returning

Rab and Billy

to the cry, 'Don't eat the yellow snow!' When we had first been in bothies I had wondered why there were so many bottles around them. I soon found out that they were not for holding candles, as first thought.

Corrour bothy is tiny. When we were there we always camped nearby and we only spent one night actually in the place, packed jammed tight on a wet, wild night when our wee tent succumbed to heavy rain. Bothies like Kinbreck had fairly clean wooden floors upstairs reached by a ladder, but a hard wood floor is still not conducive to a good night's sleep.

Today we would only consider a bothy as a last resort. Many, I feel, have become too accessible, especially to the mountainbikers – all have suffered the consequences. Places like Ryvoan and Peanmeanach and even Sourlies we have found to be used by people on drink and, more worryingly, drugs. Another bothy we declined to sleep in was Culra. It was clean enough but as it was constructed from asbestos sheeting we decided to give it a wide berth.

One thing we never forgot was that many bothies were at one time someone's home. On a walk into part of the Fisherfield Munros we stopped at a ruined bothy marked on the map as Lochivroan. It had been a wet, dismal day, but unfortunately most of the roof was by then part of the floor. What made it so poignant was that on parts of the remaining walls and roof there were pasted old catalogue adverts from before the turn of the century. Some were for Victorian fashions and others for early washing machines, tools, and farm implements. It must have been a hard and often lonely life in some of these remote glens, especially for the woman of the house.

Another bothy was almost the death of Bill and Rab. They had been walking in the Glenfinnan hills and after a jolly evening in the Lochailort Hotel had decided to make for Essan bothy for the night. They padded along the railway line in the dark feeling quite safe – after all, it was Sunday and no trains ran. Suddenly Rab, without knowing why, shouted, 'Jump, Billy! Jump!' Billy, to whom you usually have to repeat yourself endlessly, for once did as he was told. As they both stumbled off the track a big diesel train came roaring round the bend and clattered noisily past them. They had come within a whisker of death, but all Billy could say was, 'Ah've stubbed ma big toe!' Rab, his nerves shot, raved at him, 'Nivver mind yer toe! We wur nearly arrivin at the Fort stuck tae the front o yon train!'

Not even bothies were suitable to reach many of our hills. In that case, if the weather was fair we would settle for the best option of all, and that was the tent. We went through quite a few tents in our time. From cheap thin ones we used then discarded, to the heavy cotton ones which were fine for base camps, but on the hill we used just the flysheets and slept in the best bower of all, the heather. The most memorable campsites were on summits, not for the spectacular sunsets or sunrises but to escape the cursed midges – many a time we abandoned a good campsite with them in pursuit.

These days as we tackle the Corbetts we camp at official camping sites. Here we can make use of the facilities such as showers, and airbeds can be used for comfort. Also, rather than use the small tent, we now use a slightly larger one which allows us to cook inside away from the elements and to spread about wet gear. Once or twice as we left sites we were asked what size tent we had and we would reply, 'Och, jist a two-man tent.' Which was the truth – except that it is about twenty-odd feet long, eight feet wide and nearly five in height.

Another type of hill shelter was the 'howff'. I suppose the most well known was the Shelter Stone in the Cairngorms. I was not at ease dossing there – there was just too much human dirt and filth for our liking. We have spent nights in many a rough place but before we could use the Shelter Stone we had to remove a lot of human dirt which we felt should not have been there. Another factor was the sudden change of weather that occurred – I was mindful of the two walkers MacKenzie and Ferrier who perished trying to walk out from here over Cairngorm in 1933. It was the same on visits to Corrour, where we recalled the Barrie and Baird tragedy of 1928. We were always mindful of these events even though they happened long before we went to the hills. Another famous howff was the caves at Arrochar. We only visited them, and marvelled at the old-timers who used them in the days of the depression. We ourselves never had any need to use them: they were of another time and generation long gone.

Fortunately we never got into any serious trouble on the hills We were of the opinion that if anything happened you got yourself out of trouble. We never, ever told anyone where we were going as often we changed our plans on the hill. This was the mistake wee Billy made on a sponsored walk on the Mamores. He told the warden at Glen Nevis his route and plan for the day, but in the event he was benighted on the hills and spent a night in a survival bag. He was awakened the next morning by a Sea King helicopter hovering above him, having been alerted by the hostel warden. This sort of thing we never felt was fair to put onto anyone's shoulders.

The nearest that I ever got to coming to grief was on a day out with the Glasgow HF. After a day on the Drumochter hills I collapsed, unconscious, on the coach going home. I came to in

The HF club cottage

Pitlochry as I was being put into an ambulance to be taken to the local cottage hospital. It was not the first time this had happened – I had passed out three or four times while weight training at a gym. My doctor diagnosed that I had a grumbling appendix and told me not to worry. However, in October 1995, near the end of a long day on five Corbetts in the Auch Glen/Glen Lyon area, I began to feel very unwell and only just managed to make it back to the car, feeling awful. Late that night I had severe stomach pain and in the morning after the doctor was called I was taken into hospital with acute appendicitis.

Perhaps the best accommodation we used was a combination of bothy and hostel. This was the old HF club cottage located near

Auch Farm. It sat beside the West Highland Line and was originally a railway cottage. Towering above it was the massive bulk of Ben Dorain. Although we often used it as a centre for our climbing, it was when we used the cottage in the days between Christmas and New Year – which we did for several years – that we had our best times. On our way there we would stop on Loch Lomondside to cut firewood. The cars were left at Bridge of Orchy station and we walked the rest of the way. Our packs were always heavily loaded with coal and drink. If we ran out of drink we walked out to Bridge of Orchy hotel, and if the coal ran down we would fill up our packs at a nearby farm in Glen Dochart.

Very seldom on these festive trips did we go near a hill, but on one rare occasion we made it to the summit of Ben Mhannach at the top of Auch Glen. It was here, standing at the cairn, as wee Jimmy and I were taking our bearings in thick mist, that the rest of the boys inexplicably walked off into the mist, following the footprints in the snow of previous climbers. I can still see Jimmy jumping up and down, raging and cursing, 'The bastards! The bastards! They're always daein this tae me!' After he calmed down we decided that, well, they were grown-ups and could look after themselves, so we came back off the hill. As we got to the floor of the glen I had a stop and found a penny whistle at the bottom of my rucksack. I began playing away. The tunes echoed back and forth in the glen. It was not long before we could see the lads sheepishly coming round the mountainside, while I played 'The Hen's March Tae the Midden'.

Cooking was always interesting, especially with the Paisley men as they nearly all cooked for themselves. On one exceptional occasion when we all pooled our tins of Heinz soup into one huge pot, the only one to abstain was the president, George, who cried out in indignation, 'Ah'm no pittin ma guid Baxters Cock-a Leekie soup in wae your cheap soups!' I made porridge one time and one time only. Even the frugal Buddies balked at it. I thought it was all right – after all, I always thought that it had to be thick enough to cut with a knife. They said it wouldn't come out of the pot and that a good saw was required.

Lighting the cottage cooker was no easy task. Once when wee Stukky was attempting to light the oven and almost inside with his head and shoulders there was a flash and almighty bang. As he stood up and the smoke began to clear we could see that he looked like a black and white minstrel. His smoking hair was standing on end and his eyebrows had gone.

One year, instead of the club cottage, we all went to the 'Preesident's' room and kitchen at Tighnabruaich. Being the unpaid north chapter of the Glenniffer, and therefore at the bottom of the club's pecking order, Rab and I were allocated the floor in the living room to sleep on, while the paid-up members were allowed to sleep in beds. It had been a bitterly cold spell and all the rooms were well below freezing, with thick ice forming inside all the windows – yet unknown to the cost-conscious Paisley men, Rab and I slept with our heads near the gas fire which we kept on all night, while the others shivered in their soft beds.

Up Helly Aa

EARLY ONE SATURDAY, JIMMY Gallagher and George McCall came over to Yoker and parked Jimmy's car at my place. We all then set off north, up the old A82 heading for Strathcarron station 187 miles away. Here we parked the car at the hotel and set off to backpack into Bernais or 'Bareknees' bothy, a four-hour walk away. Arriving at the bothy we found the place empty and comparatively clean; we even got a fire going to round off the day. Next day after an early start we all crossed the nearby burn and headed across the glen to ascend Bidean Coire Sheasgaich – we called it Bidean Coire Cheesecake. The going was quite hard work through fairly deep snow. On the summit there was little to

On the summit of Bidean Choire Cheesecake

be seen in an all-white landscape. With little delay we pushed on to the next hill that day, Lurg Mhor, which we soon topped. However, an attempt to continue on to a further top proved too difficult in deep snow and whiteout conditions where we could not see how far the snow cornices overhung. And so we retreated, descending south-east and clear of the snow line to a good track and heading back to Bernais.

On the way back Rab and Jimmy went off the track to investigate another likely bothy. George and myself carried on, and found a wrecked dinghy which we all eventually managed to carry back to the bothy. Just like an Up Helly Aa, this provided us with a blazing fire, an essential element for long nights in a bothy. George later commented that it was lucky that the fumes from the paint and varnish did not poison us. As usual Rab and I had a substantial meal: Jimmy was happy enough to mess around with his smelly paraffin stove making wattery soup. George tucked into a Paisley delicacy, the famous 'Wattson's skwerries' (square sausage). He rounded his meal off with apple strudel – he couped it over the dirty bothy floor but insisted that it was too good to waste: he swept it up off the floor back into his plate one flake at a time, pecking away like some old chicken. For afters George treated us all to his wife Mergrit's home-made jam, with the words, 'Ye kin hae as much as ye like!' (Using a two-pronged fork to spread the very wattery jam, it was obvious we were not going to get much.)

Next morning following a comfortable night we set off, after a good breakfast and a tidy-up, to walk back out to Strathcarron. It took three hours this time and at the hotel we had a meal and a pint before setting off for home. As a postscript to this trip, it was once we got out that we heard the news of the disaster at Chernobyl in Russia, and that we had been in the path of the fall-out that was spread across Europe and Scotland that weekend. On later outings those of us who were there at the time were ribbed about glowing in the dark.

The Rough Bounds by Moonlight

BY FRIDAY 20 JULY BOTH Rab and I had been working away for weeks on an old Taiwan trawler called Zakanaka, laying hot pitch in the deck seams. That evening about seven we drove north heading for the West Highlands. It was, after all, midsummer. We had a late stop for a pint at the Tomdoun Hotel before continuing on to the road's end at Kinloch Hourn where we arrived at midnight. In the wee small hours we set off along the Rough Bounds of Knoydart, our way lit by a pale moon. The path wound its way up and down along the shore of the loch. As we approached Barrisdale Bay with the ruins of the old church looming before us we were startled by red deer running past. They had been foraging along the shoreline when we disturbed them.

About four in the morning we put the tent up near the bothy and gratefully crawled into our sleeping bags for a good sleep. We would probably have lain on late were it not for the bright sunlight streaming through the tent walls. On looking outside we saw that others had followed us along the track, arriving later. Our climb for the day was Larven. Setting off along the shore we walked round the bay to begin the climb up into the Coire Dhorchaill. This corrie must have been a place of high pasture at some time, with the lush grazing and the ruins of high summer sheilings. The ascent soon took us on to a more defined ridge which began to lead onto the summit of Larven. From the summit we had views looking across to Skye and the Islands and to the north across to Sgritheall on the mainland. We could also look back along the shore of Loch Hourn and across to Loch Nevis. Most importantly we could see before us our route off the mountain. This was along a long serrated and undulating ridge. And it was nice to see, as Larven is a mountain which presents the navigator with magnetic interference with the compass.

The descent from Larven on this, the sunniest and hottest day so far that year, was long and weary. We were particularly grateful to reach the Mam Barrisdale path near to where we had met it on a previous trip. On a stunning evening we arrived back at the tent around eight o'clock. After a lie-in next morning we eventually packed up and walked back out the way we had come, with a dry, hot day before us. It was on the path I met a big Englishman who asked where we were headed. I replied that we were off to see England get gubbed by Argentina in the World Cup that same day – which we did!

Glen Derry, Cairngorms

ON FRIDAY 11 JULY, Gleniffer club members George, Andy, Jimmy and Rab met as usual at my place. Jimmy left his car in my drive and we all set off north, crammed into two cars. Our aim was to walk into the Cairngorms and climb some of the big hills there. When we arrived at the Linn o' Dee we parked the cars and set off to walk into Glen Lui, carrying full packs as we were camping. On reaching the old Derry Lodge we crossed the Derry burn near the mountain rescue post and turned into Glen Derry. This lower part of the glen is fairly well forested with old Caledonian pine trees. The glen itself is a through route and part of the Larig an Laoigh (the pass of the calves). In the past it was one of the great droving routes of Scotland. Heavily laden with our packs, we all climbed up slowly into the glen and where it widens out we crossed over the burn and set up camp among a few old pine trees. There was a plentiful supply of old wood and we soon had a good fire going. With red deer grazing on the nearby slopes of Derry Cairngorm we had a grand evening round a rare fire which at times threatened to set the nearby tents alight.

An early start saw us set off straight up Derry Cairngorm. We left the tents there, only carrying day packs. A slow ascent was made up to the south ridge, the only sounds being the distant roaring of red deer and the occasional nearby belching of Andy Murdoch. The ridge was reached at point 1,040 metres, where we turned right to ascend to the summit of Derry. This was our first Munro of the day and now we swung north-east to take in the first of seven tops. The first top looks into the top half of Glen Derry where the fords of Avon lie. Below us lay the corrie that runs up to Loch Etchachan where the Hutchison Memorial hut sits. A swing to the left brought us to the top Creagan a Coire Etchachan. From here we turned away to follow round the lip of Coire Sputan Dearg which lies on the lower slopes of the Ben MacDhui massif. Instead of heading with George, Andy and

Jimmy directly to the summit of Ben MacDhui, Rab and I left them and headed for Sron Riach which commands MacDhui's southern tip overlooking the Larig Ghru.

It remained dull and cool with reasonable visibility for the whole day. Retracing our route for a short distance we now made our way to the day's biggest hill. The summit of MacDhui is well strewn with cairns. However, there is no mistaking the actual top and it was here we gathered for a photo in the mist. On this occasion there was not just one Grey Man on MacDhui – there were five of us. From the summit we set off along the tourist route from Cairngorm which is a well-worn and cairned path. We

Looking into Loch Avon
from above Shelter Stone Crag

remained on this track till the next top where we took a bearing north-east over featureless terrain on the plateau. As we descended clear of the mist we could see on our right Loch Etchachan below us.

Our next top was Carn Etchachan which overlooks the deep hollow in which Loch Avon lies. From this airy viewpoint we could look straight down and could just make out the Shelter Stone howff far below. A rough descent took us to the path below.

Instead of following the path we crossed it and again began to climb, winding round two more tops and then on to the third Munro of the day, Beinn Mheadhoin – a strange summit. On the top there are huge granite tors which look as though they were placed as the backdrop of a western movie. On the highest tor are rounded hollows: supposedly as the story goes they were used as part of some fertility rites – who knows?

Retracing our tracks to the previous col, we then took in the last top of the day. The last descent of the day, down a rough, steep hillside, brought us onto the track we had met earlier. From here we turned down the glen, stopping briefly to look into the Hutchison Hut which at that time was little more than a hovel open to the elements. A short distance from here the track contours round the hillside to meet the through track from the Larig an Lui. Soon we were back at the campsite and preparing our evening meal. Once again we lit a huge fire around which we sat resting after one very hard day in which we took in three Munros and seven tops.

Another early morning rise, this time dull and misty, saw us on the way again. This time we crossed the burn and went straight up the other side of the glen to climb Craig Derry (a top) and on to the summit of Beinn Bhreac. From here we could hear the distant sound of gunfire and wondered where it was coming from – it was still early for stalking but the shooting seems to take place all year. A long trudge over flat moorland took us on to our last top and Munro, Beinn a Chaorainn Beag and Beinn a Chaorainn. The summit cairn of Beinn a Chaorainn has a navvy's pickaxe-head embedded in it. From here we began the last descent into the east side of the Larig an Lui path which took us back to the campsite. As the day was still early George and Andy decided to walk out to the Linn and head for home. Rab, Jimmy and I took the opportunity to spend another night here since it had turned out nice again. So again we built up a huge fire and enjoyed another night with the glen to ourselves. With a lie-in next morning we quietly broke camp and leisurely trekked out to the Linn o' Dee and a good run home

Corrour Bothy, Cairngorms

WITH THE GLENIFFER TEAM we met at Yoker and then drove north up the A9 to the Braemar area and parked at the Linn o' Dee. In the party were myself, Rab Doyle, George McCall, Andy Murdoch, Jimmy Gallagher and Stukky Stirling. We walked in to Derry Lodge and as we set off a red squirrel ran across the road, almost tripping up wee Stukky. When we reached the old lodge building we could see that since we were last there the place had really fallen into a ruinous state. When the Paisley boys got to Derry Lodge they decided to doss in the building rather than bother about erecting the tents they were carrying. Rab and I had a look around the building. Disgusted to find much evidence of human waste we decided to pitch the tent and camp nearby.

In the morning we awoke to a wet misty day. When the others got themselves together we set off up Glen Luibeg. This was where Rab Scott the well-known keeper lived and where his bothy stood – it had recently been burned. Winding our way up the glen we soon found ourselves at the foot of Carn A' Mhaim. Just up from the path we left our packs and climbed this Munro. Carn A' Mhaim stands just to the south of Ben MacDhui and overlooks the Larig Ghru track. When we came off we collected the packs and made our way into the Larig Ghru, heading for Corrour bothy. Corrour is an old keeper's hut and offers the only shelter for miles around. Again the Gleniffer refused to camp despite humping big, heavy tents, and plumped to use the bothy. Of course we decided to camp – after all, sleeping in the heather is always more comfortable than a hard stone floor. After a meal in the cramped bothy we settled down in the tent. However, during the night it began to rain heavily. Our trusty old Vango was leaking badly. We were forced to concede defeat and retreat to the bothy. I can recall standing looking out of the door across the glen, with the mist down to about one hundred feet, and seeing a big yellow Wessex helicopter heading down the Larig towards

Braemar, its searchlight showing the way.

This night the bothy was full to the brim. Cooking on the small table and tying to get around the tiny fireplace strewn with wet clothes was time-consuming and demanded much patience. A few people looked in but when they saw and heard us they soon moved on. Two soldiers stopped by to cook a meal. There was one tall guy with an enormous pack and a little guy with a slightly smaller one. The big fella pulled tin after tin of canned food from

The leaky tent

the depths of this huge bag. I never saw so much grub in one bag – how he managed to carry such a load I'll never know. Later when we were all packed tight in our sleeping bags and ranged the length of the wall like the seven dwarfs we did our best to sleep comfortably on such a hard concrete floor. George had carried in an inflatable airbed for comfort but had cut down the amount of food to compensate. We were packed so tight that you had to lie on your back: to lie on your side was too painful on the old hipbones. So there we lay. The snorers were soon in business – anyone passing would have thought there were motorbikes and chainsaws in operation, accompanied by various whistlings from soprano, bass and treble Armenian nose flutes.

Dull and misty was the weather next morning when we awoke after a night on the hard floor. Stiff as boards, like the old men we were, we jostled around the tiny dwelling preparing our breakfasts. Shortly we were following the track behind the bothy as we set off to climb the Devil's Point. The Devil's Point or the Devil's Penis overlooks the bothy and dominates the bottom of the Larig. The old-timers, many of whom worked in shipyards, described the big granite slabs of this hill as boiler plates, and on a wet day with water running off them that's just what they looked like. After reaching the summit up a fairly well-defined path we retraced our steps to the col and then continued up and on to Cairn Toul. From the summit we could see into the corrie with Lochan Uaine directly below us looking like a piece of slate lying in the corrie.

Continuing along the ridge over Sgor an Lochan Uaine, which means the Angel's Peak, we navigated along the tops to the next summit in mist – to our right there were seemingly sheer drops into the corries below. However, from this next top, marked as 1,265 metres, we were now on the flat arctic-like plateau that typifies the terrain in the Cairngorms. On the east side the deep trough of the Larig Ghru; on the west, steep slopes into Glen Einich. As we made our way to Einich Cairn we came upon the Pools of Dee where the river of that name begins. Still in mist we now headed for our last Munro of the day, Braeriach. This was where out of the mist loomed a small group of reindeer. They were not afraid of us, like red deer, and were looking to be hand-fed. We all began to reach for our cameras to capture them on film. With their velvet antlers and white markings around their ankles they looked like a bunch of lost golfers. As wee Jimmy tried to photograph one it kept walking towards him. As he backed away he eventually fell on his backside. Much to the amusement of the rest of us.

From Braeriach we soon began to descend into the Larig Ghru. Dropping out of the mist we could see down to Corrour with the distinct shape of the Devil's Point. We came upon large pieces of aluminium. I believe this was the wartime wreck of an RAF Anson.

Once down in the floor of the Larig we picked up the well-worn path to walk back down the glen to the bothy.

Down in the glen you become aware of the immensity of the surrounding mass of mountains that hems you in. We passed by the Clach nan Taillear, or the Tailors' Boulder, where three drunken tailors perished, foolishly trying to cross the pass one winter for a wager. As we drew level with the bothy the path cut off down to the bridge: you have to cross here to reach the bothy. This bridge was erected in the 1950s by the Cairngorm Mountaineering Club. In all the times I have passed through this glen the river Dee was never low enough to make a safe crossing to reach the shelter of the bothy, so tantalisingly near.

The evening began to clear away with pleasant sunshine and the hidden mountains all around us revealed. Ben MacDhui stood out clear as a bell, and towering above the bothy the boiler plates of the Devil's Point glistened in the sun. Rab and I decided to put the tent back up and chance a good night's sleep. Early next morning, well refreshed after a comfortable and peaceful night, we awoke to a bright, sunny day. The side of the glen where we were camped was still in shade and was cold. The boys all posed for photos outside the bothy and on the bridge before we set off with heavy packs. Our route was south along the Larig which begins to open out. However, we were only going a short distance. Our target for the day was to climb two Munros, Beinn Bhrotain (or, as we say, Ben Rotten) and Monadh Mor. These two hills are set back from the Larig Ghru overlooking Glen Geusachan, the glen of the pines – a wild and lonely place with a tributary of the River Dee running through it. The floor of the glen is littered with the skeletal white-bleached remains of old Caledonian pine trees. To reach the glen we were faced with a double river crossing. We had only a short distance of the Dee in which to make a decision before it joined the river coming out of Geasachan. The boys were keen to get on over but Rab pointed out that where it was narrow it was also deep and icy cold, being so high up.

A decision was made to cross at the only fairly wide part we could find. Each one of us had to decide whether to cross barefoot or just with boots on, and to roll up trousers or take them off and keep them dry. I think we all opted to strip off and go barefoot: that is, all except wee Jimmy who triumphantly fished from the depths of his Brown Bess rucksack a pathetic little pair of black gym shoes which looked like a pair of ballet dancer's pumps. He must have carried them around in the bottom of his pack for years just waiting for this opportunity to wear them, of course amid much ribald banter.

One river crossing is bad enough but two were bloody awful.

Preparing to walk out to Linn of Dee

With bare toes and legs suddenly going numb, trying to steady yourself and keep upright while holding a heavy pack above your head is not a nice experience. Wee Stukky Stirling was having difficulty crossing: Rab went back to help him over so I think he did about three crossings in total. Once across the two streams amid much loud roaring and bawling, we rubbed some life into bruised toes and frozen feet before continuing up the glen.

A direct assault was to be made on Bhrotain. Leaving the packs we went straight up, no messing around. I can recall looking back and seeing Rab Doyle pushing wee Stukky up by his bum. With no pack to slow us we were soon at the top and savouring the views all around. Everywhere we looked were the big blue peaks of the Cairngorms. In Glasgow speak, it was 'pure dead brilliant'. From Bhrotain it was down and up on to Monadh Mor. Although 1,113 metres in height, set among this part of the Gorms this is a mere plook of a hill.

Retracing our steps to the bealach between the two hills we made our descent back into the glen and eventually retrieved the bags. Here we prepared for the march out to Linn of Dee. By this time we were all tired. The boys were cursing the heavy tents they packed but didn't use. In carrying the tents we all had brought bare rations and now a good belly-buster was needed to see us out to the road end. As the boys repacked heavy sacks and George went skinny-dipping (you would have thought that the cold river crossing was enough for anyone), Rab and I pulled from our bags a meal that had the others slavering. It was merely bread, potatoes and a tin of meatballs but at that time and place it was a veritable feast.

As we set off we were now on the wrong side of the Dee. It was too deep and fast-flowing to attempt another crossing and as we had a fairly good path to follow we hiked the three or four miles to where the Larig joins the route from Glen Tilt at White Bridge. Just before the bridge we passed the Chest of Dee, a series of small waterfalls where Rab and I had stopped on a walk at Easter 1978, when we had sat eating Easter eggs. The rest of the walk out proved uneventful, apart from for wee Jimmy. As he was hoisting on his huge Brown Bess pack, the shoulder strap broke. This was a bag that many of the guys had bought at a sale. These bags were huge but the straps were too wide for comfortable carrying and were attached to the bag by a tiny metal key ring. This had snapped and it was lucky for Jimmy that the walk was almost over. The going was on a fairly flat road all the way back to the Linn of Dee where we had parked our cars. This was one of wee Stukky Stirling's last big outings with the boys. He had found it difficult to carry a large pack and, unlike on previous trips, we all had our share to carry and could not make things easier for him.

In Torridon with the Mujahedin

ON TUESDAY 2 SEPTEMBER, four of the Gleniffer team rendez-voused with Rab Doyle and myself at Yoker. In two cars we left at one in the afternoon to drive north to Loch Torridon youth hostel. Late that afternoon as we turned into Glen Torridon and passed by Loch Clare we were confronted by the brooding mass of Liathach (The Grey One) filling the skyline. The enormity of our task subdued our high spirits as we drove the last few miles to the hostel.

The next day on a fine and sunny morning we used the two cars to ferry the party along to our start at the east end of Beinn Eighe and ensure that we had a car waiting at the finish. Our climb began at Cromasaig with a long approach up the Allt a'Chuirn burn. Our first peak of the day, Sgurr a'Fhir Duibh, was reached after a long slog and a short but steep climb up the south-east ridge to its top. Gathering together we followed the ridge south then west to Sgurr Ban. The whole ridge was very rocky under-foot, but this stretch was particularly tricky in parts as the rock was loose and unstable, and in places we had to look for hand-holds. It was with a huge sigh of relief that we eventually passed Sgurr Ban onto ground just as rough but much easier to walk on.

Our next top was Spidean Coire nan Clach. From here on the terrain took on the aspect of big, bare, rocky mountains not unlike Afghanistan or Morocco. We ourselves added to the scene, looking the part of Mujahedin, especially Rab Alexander in his headgear and Andy Murdoch wearing my mother's hand-knitted tea cosy on his head. In the far distance, looming closer with every peak that we passed, was the towering mass of Liathach, which end-on looked totally impossible to scale. However, we still had much to do before we met that challenge. From A' Choinnich Mhor we turned off the main ridge to walk out to scale the peak of Ruadh Stac Mhor, the Munro of Beinn Eighe. When we reached the top we had a good break for lunch. To the north of us was the whole of the Ben Eighe forest. Only there was not a tree in sight – just the vista of grey mountains set against a blue sky and sparkling lochs. Retracing our steps back to the main ridge we began to head west again, set to bag our last top, Sail Mhor.

As we swung left from the top to avoid the cliffs of Coire Mich Fhearchair we came upon aircraft wreckage. This was the remains of a Canadian Maritime reconnaissance Lancaster which crashed on a training flight in the 1950s with no survivors. 'Poor bastards,' we thought – a mere twelve feet or so higher and they would have cleared the ridge. Most of the fuse-lage had fallen into the corrie and was at the time deemed too dangerous to recover. Pushing on from the crash site we quickly came upon a rather difficult 'bad'

Mujahedin on Ben Eighe?

step which we shorter ones had problems getting down. Once beyond this, however, we quickly bashed on to gain the last peak of the day. With there being no point in trying to go back over the bad step onto higher ground we opted to retrace our steps a little way along the ridge then drop straight off long, steep but mainly grassy slopes to the glen, Coire Dubh, below. This was a knee-jerker of a descent, but once we reached the floor of the glen we were relieved to find that we had a good path to follow out to the road where we had a car parked at Loch an Tasgaich.

Later, back at the hostel, we settled down to a big meal washed down with copious amounts of wine. The hostel that night was very hot and stuffy. Unable to open the windows due to the presence of the dreaded midge, we had to endure not only the heat also the roar of the snorers.

The next day we set off along the Diabeg road to a small car park at the mouth of Coire Mhic Nobuil. This was to be a very wet and extremely windy day. We pushed on up the well-trod track where we turned north onto the south-east ridge of Sgurr Mhor of Ben Alligin. Now exposed to the strong winds I began to be buffeted around, increasingly spooked by being blown off my feet. This was also very tiring. I decided enough was enough. Not giving the others a chance to change my mind I turned back and came off the ridge while they, completely unaware, battled on up to go round the 'Horns of Alligin'.

Back down in the glen, not wishing to waste the day completely, I decided to make an attempt to climb Liathach from the west side. If the rest of the week's weather went to pieces at least I would have climbed part of Liathach. So up I went, climbing solo. I find that on your own you tend to push harder, and this I did. On this side of the mountain I was sheltered from the worst of the wind. It was dull but visibility was not too bad. Slogging straight up from the glen I gained the ridge just to the east of Sgurr a'Chadail at 700 metres. The ridge is not wide here but soon broadens as it climbs towards the steeper slopes of Mullach an Rathain. As I ascended this slope to the summit I could look straight down to the hostel and buildings at Torridon. This looked a possible if not long and steep way off. When I reached the summit I did not linger very long before turning about to make my way off. My descent followed the whole of the west ridge back into the mouth of the glen where we all started from. With time to look about I could see good views of Loch Torridon in the late afternoon sun, while to my right I was almost looking down on the nearby Beinn Dearg, a Corbett just short of Munro height – a long, narrow hill with no obvious way up onto it. Bashing on, I made good time back to where we had started and met up with the others coming off their hill. They were none too pleased with me. My defection had broken all the rules, and I had missed a Munro and ended up doing a much bigger day.

That night back at the hostel we were all more subdued. For the next day the weather did not look too promising to tackle the Liathach from the east side. From the east Liathach is a fearsome-looking mountain and appears completely unscalable. Sleep was hard to come by that night as we lay in the heat listening to the snorers and worrying about the morrow.

Next morning with a hearty breakfast and ensuring a good supply of liquids we prepared for what looked likely to be a warm day. Repeating the previous day's start we soon had everyone ferried along to the start of the climb in Glen Torridon. Rather than going right to the end of the mountain we started up where there was a notch on the skyline above us between the two easterly tops. This was probably the most difficult part of the day, climbing up a faint path on ever steepening ground. Liathach has layers of grassy terraces and short, almost vertical cliffs from top to bottom. It was up through this that our path eventually led us on to the narrow ridge. Here we turned to the right and a short walk took us to our first top, Stuc a'Choire Dhuibh Bhig. A mite cooler after our slog up, we were soon pulling on more layers of clothing.

Before us lay the whole ridge with summits and tops and the path running along the top. Over to the right lay the mass of Beinn Eighe, looking much lower. Ahead as we approached was the main summit of Spidean a'Choire Leith rising above us. A short easy-looking ridge runs from this top but ends in a vertical drop. Not the place to make a mistake in mist. On reaching the top of this peak we had our break and a good breather. Liathach was not as fearsome as we had thought, but before us there still lay the Fasserin Pinnacles – not unlike the Aonach Eagach in Glencoe but shorter in length.

As a precaution George had brought with him a rope and some slings just in case we had any problems negotiating this airy part of the ridge. Unfortunately he decided that, rather than scramble along them, he would take a rough deer-track traversing along the side of the mountain just below the pinnacles. However, he forgot to give us the ropes and slings, leaving the rest of us to scramble along astride the ridge without them. The pinnacles as it turned out were exciting enough but not as difficult as we thought. George, on the other hand, had experienced a more nerve-wracking time going along the sides, as the path was non-existent in many places.

The next summit was quickly topped, probably due to an

Liatach from Ben Eighe

adrenaline rush on the pinnacles. This was Mullach an Rathain – my second visit to it in two days. As we sat languishing at the cairn Rab and Jimmy were considering an attempt on the northern pinnacles, the north top of this peak. After some deliberation they and Rab Alexander decided to go for it. With little else to do the rest of us settled down to watch the show as the three of them slowly inched their way out on to the poorly defined top. By the slow progress they were making it was clear that the rock was loose and rotten. We could occasionally observe the figures below throwing off tufts of grass and rocks. Finally they went out as far as they thought to make the top count and then slowly began to make their way back to us on the summit. At length they joined us at the cairn and we set off down the west ridge and back to the hostel.

Next morning, George, Bobby Alexander and Andy headed for home. I ran Rab and Jimmy along Glen Torridon for a through walk of Coire Mhic Nobuil while I set off for the other end to climb Ben Alligin on my own. Setting off from the car park I climbed swiftly up into the corrie of Tom na Gruagaich. The path here winds steeply up through large rocks and boulders and emerges on the ridge. This I soon scaled and with a nice warm, sunny day in prospect I was making excellent time over the tops of Alligin. Passing the deep indent into the mountain I pushed onwards to the main top of Sgurr Mhor. Despite the stunning views I did not linger long and began to backtrack down the corrie, leaping from boulder to boulder. The boys were back at the car after a good through walk. Then it was off home with everyone well pleased with our visit to Torridon. We had climbed four Munros and nine tops with a round trip of 563 miles.

Ben Alder

ONCE AGAIN IT WAS EASTER, the defining start to our year, and for both Doyle and me the end of the Munros was almost in sight. Our objective this trip was the big, isolated mountain of Ben Alder. After familiar drag up the A9 we obtained a key from the local estate keeper in Dalwhinnie then Rab and I drove down the side of Loch Ericht on the rough road that goes in to Loch Pattack. As I parked the car near some others we noticed ponies grazing nearby. These, we had been told, liked to chew off car wing mirrors, aerials, tyres, and any other protruding parts.

Our plan was to walk down towards the bothy at Culra where we would pitch the tent. However, we saw that there were a few already there and anyway, being old shipyard workers, we were horrified to realise that the place was made from asbestos sheeting. We decided we definitely would not be sleeping inside. As it was still early in the year, up here the weather was extremely cold. Surrounded by snow-clad mountains we set up our campsite near the river called the Allt a'Chaoil Reidhe and prepared for the next day's climbing. All that we could see of a mist-covered Ben Alder was the pointed Lancet Ridge away to the south. I had been feeling unwell with a bad bout of flu. I spent a long sleepless night in my sleeping bag, drenched in sweat while shivering uncontrollably: I was almost delirious and obviously had a fever.

The next morning I awoke feeling horribly weak but the fever had gone. I forced myself to eat some breakfast and some hot tea as we zipped up the tent and prepared to face the day. Rab did his best to cheer me up and had both of us laughing, as well as keeping warm, as he performed an impromptu Morris dance, banging our metal dixies. The low grey sky above was not an encouraging start. Although very cold it was at least dry as we set off for the hill. Our plan was to climb the four Munros of Carn Dearg, Geal Charn, Aonach Beag and Beinn Eibhinn. Very quickly we found ourselves climbing in a thickening mist that swirled around, clinging to us and leaving us with hair and beards dripping wet. Climbing in this shroud was eerie – all sound smothered and absorbed in the mist. The only noise to be heard was our rasping breath as we toiled up the steep hillside. The higher we climbed the colder it became, and soon we were having great difficulty trying to scramble up over ice-covered rocks: as usual we had no crampons with us. It was only on the top halves of these hills that we found the going less slippery – though just as hard – in deep snow.

Once we gained the first summit, Carn Dearg, we traversed along over an unnamed top and a steep climb through a narrowing rocky ridge. From here on there were many corniced ridges, which were dangerous under the conditions. We were unable to see where the edges were against a dirty grey background. It was becoming more of a whiteout as the day wore on. There were to be no lunch stops, just a hot drink and a bite as we walked on. One by one the tops fell to our slow but relentless assault. Despite the conditions we were quite happy about gaining the summits, but on the last mountain we had great difficulty determining where the exact summit was – and it was only by criss-crossing the unmarked top in all directions that we decided that the top must be under a good covering of snow. Our descent was a slow one down the south ridge of Eibhinn and, once clear of the snow line, into the valley floor of the Uisge Labhair.

From here we were now faced with a good five miles or so back to the tent, but first we had to climb up to the Bealach Dubh. After we got some of our wet gear off and had the last of the food and drink we set off with the Bealach Chumhainn on our right. It was while attempting to cross over this pass heading to Ben Alder bothy that a party of five men perished on a New Year outing in 1962; the only survivor was a woman whose husband was one of those who died. With such thoughts it was not a nice place to linger so we quickly pushed on at a good pace and only slowed once we were over the pass and walking under the lee of the Lancet Ridge. There was Culra bothy in the far distance with our wee tent beyond.

That night in the tent we were two wee weary men and it was

with the realisation of how enormous a day we had done that we fell asleep in the damp misty glen. We had climbed one big Munro and walked a fair distance to three others that, although close together, had considerable drops between them.

The next morning we were too tired to make any real attempt at Ben Alder, especially as we were on the wrong side of the mountain considering the weather conditions. So we opted for a walk past Loch Pattack along the river to the bothy at Blackburn. Blackburn at that time was a huge place. Strangely for a bothy it was constructed of wood. There was plenty of firewood in the area, but sadly this bothy was burned to the ground a few years later. When we returned to the car I was relieved to find that the ponies had not eaten any tyres or wing mirrors. This ended our first attempt to bag Ben Alder and we never even got to set foot near the hill. So off we drove, bumping our way slowly along the rough road to Dalwhinnie and then home.

However, on 7 August 1988, when I had only five Munros still to do, we returned to Ben Alder. This time our approach was from the south with us leaving the car near Kinloch Rannoch. The weather on this occasion was much warmer as we sweated our way into the hills. The route was difficult to follow through dense forest and we were suffering badly under the hot sun, becoming quite disorientated. Eventually we had to admit that we were lost. The hardest, and almost always right, decision is to admit the mistake and to retrace your steps to the start and get it right. However, we were lucky in being able to rejoin the track beyond the forest, which we could have avoided in the first place. As the afternoon wore on, pursued by hordes of flies (and me with sore feet, having stupidly worn new boots without breaking them in), we eventually approached Ben Alder cottage after a few miles along the side of Loch Ericht. As we trekked along in silence the peace was broken by the sound of aircraft: into view across the loch three huge Hercules transports flying in formation began to disgorge paratroops. Just as quickly the planes were gone, leaving the parachutists to glide soundlessly to earth.

Crossing a new-looking wooden bridge we staggered thankfully the last few yards up to the bothy. It was empty and we could see that there had been some recent refurbishment work done to the place. We set down our packs in a dark, cool, new room that had been added on, with clean, new floorboards. One thing I noticed was a light bulb hanging from the ceiling and a light switch by the corner. This was someone's idea of a joke as we were miles from any electricity source. Ben Alder had been a favourite bothy of the Gleniffer boys. On one memorable occasion after a big winter's day on the hills and with a huge fire blazing away the boys were ranged all around the walls stripped to their Damart long-johns. As the night wore on they ran out of drink and some of them walked out to the hotel at Dalwhinnie just for 'merr drink'. A mere fifteen-mile round trip.

After a quiet night with the place to ourselves we awoke to a fine morning. Our first hill of the day was Ben Alder's satellite, Beinn Bheoil. Our climb, starting at six o'clock, took us straight up the burn away from the bothy. The first top we gained was Sron Coire na h-Iolaire. The route was fairly straightforward, yet the Gleniffer on a later visit in good weather came out from the bothy and went straight up the wrong hill. From the top the ridge narrowed as we plodded along to the cairn on Bheoil's summit. From here we were rewarded with excellent views all around. The length of Loch Ericht lay below us while to our east were the hills we had stumbled around in almost whiteout conditions the previous year. Directly west of us and separated by a small loch were the cliffs of Ben Alder, our next target for the day.

Retracing our steps from Bheoil we turned off down towards the Bealach Breabaig where we had a welcome drum-up before tackling Alder itself. As Rab and I toiled slowly up onto the plateau of the mountain we encountered a small group of wild goats. Unusually they did not run off on sighting us and for a while we were entertained by a pair of males having a headbutting contest. The sound of skulls clashing was all that could be heard in the otherwise still morning air. Traversing the cliffs overlooking Garbh Coire we had a short stop at the Lochan Garbh Coire before walking on to the summit cairn where we had lunch proper.

Our way back was just to about-turn and return towards the col but instead of going down to the bealach we went straight off the hill directly to the bothy. Once back at the cottage we had a wash, a good meal and a rest before we marched out to the car. We must have been feeling quite fit because I don't remember much of the walk back – only that we were still able to drive north, stopping in at the Struan Inn for a bar lunch then driving all the way along by Dalwhinnie and Lagganside to Nancy Smith's hostel at Fersit for the night.

At Fersit we spent an uncomfortably warm night in my old caravan which was now at Nancy's. Rab was demented by the midges that abounded here, his face metamorphosing through the many pained expressions that we have come to experience as he began to lose his mind . By this time Fersit had become very run down and we were only too glad to leave early the next morning. We gave Nancy a lift round to Fort William while we were heading, not for home, but to the island of Mull. At this stage in the Munro game I was down to three to do, and we were making the most of each outing, even if it meant dashing about across the country. Crossing over the ferry at Corran we bashed on through the quiet roads of Ardgour heading for Lochaline and the ferry to Fishnish. The ferry was quiet with a calm crossing. The only incident of note was another motorist bumping into the side of my car and Rab shouting at the guy. Once on the island I sped along quiet roads – this was one of the benefits of stealing away midweek. At the foot of Ben More I parked on the shore then we set off straight up the hill. As we climbed it began to cloud over and once on the summit we could see nothing, so it was back down the way we had come. It would only be on a later visit that we would see the views from this peak. When we got back to the car we wasted no time in speeding for the ferry, not wishing to spend a night on the island. On the run home our only stop was at the Inverarnan Hotel where we met two of our friends from the HF, John and Derek. We had driven over 450 miles to climb three Munros, and with two more to go the bit was now firmly between my teeth.

The Shelter Stone

ONE FRIDAY IN MAY, RAB DOYLE and Bobby Alexander rendez-voused at my place for a visit to the Cairngorms. There was a loose plan to meet up with the rest of the Gleniffer on the hills. An uneventful drive north saw us return to these hills which had always involved big club outings. Near Glenmore Lodge we parked the car and walked into Ryvoan bothy, arriving at nine after a pleasant wander through the pines of the pass of Ryvoan and by the green waters of Lochan Uaine, where we spent a poor night with no fire, sleeping on a bare wooden floor. Leaving Ryvoan early next morning we walked on into the Strath Nethy area, stopping for a break in the shelter of Bynack stables. It was dull and dry to begin with but soon deteriorated to a cold wintry day. Our first hill was Bynack Mhor, a long slog up an easy ridge. The summit and western slopes are dotted with large tors called the 'Barns of Bynack'. We stopped on the summit for lunch before doing the tops of Bynack Beag and A'Choinnich.

Across the glen Cairngorm itself was lost in mist. The rest of the Gleniffer boys were supposed to be on that hill but we never saw them. On descending to the low col that separates Bynack from Cairngorm we came across dotterel – a member of the plover family – walking about in the snow. This was the first time I had seen them and I was surprised at how tame they were. At one point you practically had to shoo them out of the way. Dropping down from this col took us to the shore of Loch Avon, one of the highest lochs in Scotland. The path took us along the north shore under the lee of the Cairngorm itself. As we rounded the top of the loch we found ourselves looking up at the surrounding heights at the head of the corrie.

Above us began to loom the massive Shelter Stone crags where we could see a jumble of giant rock lying at its foot. Among this pile of debris we located our howff for the night, the famous Shelter Stone, which we knew from photographs – especially photos that wee Billy Billings had taken some decades previously and was endlessly casting up to us. The area surrounding the Stone was covered in human filth from the previous winter and many decades before. Inside, or rather under, the Stone itself it was very dirty: before we could use the place we had to clean it out. While we were doing this Bob Alexander decided to go off and climb a Munro almost straight above us. With a good path we were happy to let him go do his own thing.

Bobby and Rab at the Shelter Stone howff

While we stayed at the Stone we heard the beat of a helicopter and soon saw a large Sea King buzzing about close under the cliffs. At one point he flew over us and by sign asked if we were OK. Soon the howff was habitable and after a meal we settled down for a night under the Stone. At some point both Rabs must have seen the resident rodent: I certainly didn't but it must have upset Bobby as he had a bad night's sleep. Either that or he found it uncomfortable to sleep under a rock weighing several hundred tons – unlike Rab and I he probably never worked in the bilges of a tanker or bulk carrier and he was claustrophobic. Also I must be one of the few people who could almost stand upright underneath it.

We woke early next morning. It was quite a bit colder and when we looked outside there had been a fresh fall of snow. Bobby tried for ages to boil some eggs but it was just too cold. This change in the weather was a sign not to linger, so at about eight we departed and retraced our steps the way we came. On rounding Loch Avon we climbed back up to the saddle but instead of climbing over Bynack we made our way along Strath Nethy in mist, passing the stables and out through the pass of Ryvoan and by the Green Lochan to the car at Glenmore. It must have been colder than we had thought because unusually the car proved difficult to start. Our drive home and dropping Bobby Alexander at Glasgow airport was a round trip of 320 miles.

'Munros, aye! Taps – nivver!'

ON THE NIGHT OF JUNE 19, our by now customary madcap midsummer outing was to walk in to climb the two Munros of the eastern Cairngorms, Beinn a'Bhuird and Ben Avon, along with their many tops – a long walk in to remote and very high hills. Unusually for us Rab and I drove north late that Friday afternoon, hoping to avoid heavy traffic. The Gleniffer team had all left earlier and we had planned to meet up with them. When we arrived at the old Invercauld bridge by Braemar we found that the boys had parked their cars and gone on ahead. With our hefty packs, and the tent split between us, we set off at a slow pace to follow them, first past Invercauld House and then up into Gleann an t-Sluggain.

Earlier that day Rab had been lifting concrete slabs in his garden and had pulled a muscle in his back so carrying a heavy pack made for slow and painful progress throughout most of this outing. He had to lie down and rest every twenty minutes or so. After about three miles we were surprised to come upon the boys with the tents set up for the night. We had thought that they were going to do the same as us and just forget the clock and habit, making the most of the long midsummer daylight hours. Obviously, being creatures of habit, they were going to make this their base camp and travel light the next day. So after some good-natured banter we shuffled on, determined to make a good show.

Near to the top of the glen we came to the ruin of the old Sluggain Lodge, its stark ruined walls outlined against the western skyline. Beyond these ruins the track dropped slightly and we soon turned off it to cross the upper reaches of the Quoich Water. Barefoot we waded into the cold fast-flowing water, weighed down with the cumbersome packs. Halfway across I stumbled on the slippery rocks and fell in. Struggling out onto the far side, soaked and with Rab's back suffering from his exertions in crossing, we decided to just get the tent up there and then in the deep heather. We were not too disappointed – we would certainly have liked to walk all night as we had planned, but here we were well into the hills and at the foot of the first one. We settled down for a few hours' sleep on a comfy bed of heather.

About dawn it was still very light. We had a drum-up and broke camp, and slowly set off onto the hill. We struggled in the heather up Carn Fiaclach, the south-east ridge of the south top of Beinn a'Bhuird. Our progress was slow but the weather was dull and dry. Soon the slope eased and the heather got shorter, and before

On the Eastern Cairngorms

long we were on the summit at 1,177 metres. From here we looked back for any sign of the boys but we could see nothing of them. So onwards on a good high-level ridge we headed north for the main summit just over a mile away along the ridge with deep corries gouged into the mountain's eastern side. Suddenly we could hear the unmistakable thump thump of a helicopter close by, but we could see no sign, even though the visibility was not too bad. Suddenly a huge yellow Sea King rose from out of the depths of the corrie near A'Chioch. It had been manoeuvring below us out of sight.

Upon reaching the north top, the first Munro of the day, we sat down for a welcome rest. The heavy packs were taking their toll, and with Rab's back giving him pain we considered a retreat off the hills from a low part of the ridge known as the 'Sneck', a possible escape route. However, this was still beyond another top, Cnap a'Chleirich. As we prepared to set off again the boys hove into view and in no time caught up with us. It was just like the hare and the tortoise. They had left their tents to travel light, but they were committed to returning to the campsite which was by now miles away. Rab and I on the other hand, carrying our homes on our backs like snails, could make camp anywhere we pleased. After the usual insults the team jogged off and were soon out of sight. When we reached Cnap a'Chleirich (1,162 metres) we struck off the main ridge to the north top of Stob an t-Sluichd, about a mile away, trudging out to it and back again. Once back on the main ridge the way now dropped into the Sneck. From here we could have turned off with one good Munro in the bag but we decided to keep going, albeit at a slow pace.

A breather on the col saw us pulling ourselves up the grassy slopes of Ben Avon. Once on the ridge, instead of going for the summit we turned south to head for two outlying tops. The furthest away one had a considerable drop to it and as we were coming back this way we took a chance and left the packs near the top of the ridge. This was a good move as we made excellent time out to Carn Eas and back. Despite this reprieve we were beginning to tire by now. The walk along the ridge to the summit peak of Ben Avon, Leabaidh an Daimh Bhuidhe, although fairly easy going, was done at a slower pace. Ben Avon's summit came and went as we plodded wearily on. The mist had rolled in and we were now using the compass.

At the Mullach Lochan nan Gobhar the ridge divides. A decision was made to miss out the top of Clach Choutsaich and to head instead for the northernmost tops. In the sheltered side of a massive tor we stopped for a rest and to brew up some soup. As we sat in the mist with the stove hissing away we could suddenly hear voices coming closer. Surely it wasn't the boys? Yes, indeed it was. From the mist they emerged, just as surprised to see us. No longer did they kid us on. They were knackered, and with the best of the day gone due to the mist they were a long way from their campsite. As we all parted once more, now heading in opposite directions, George was heard to mutter wearily, 'Munros, aye! Taps – nivver!'

Much revived by our drum-up and cheered at the team's discomfort we made good time over the last two tops of the day. Turning off East Meue Gorm Craig, we descended quickly down easy slopes and headed east over open moorland to hit a path at the north end of Loch Builg. We walked the length of this lonely loch. It seems this loch contains a species of char, a fish left over from the Ice Age. At the end of the loch we left the path and made camp on a flat green area beside the ruins of Loch Builg Lodge. Thankful to be off the hills after a long, weary day we relaxed with a hot meal in this wild lonely place. Lying in the tent that night we could hear snipe flying around, their wings whirring. There were other sounds too: when we awoke later we realised that the area was teeming with big blue mountain hares.

When we broke camp that morning we had a seven-mile walk out to the car. The morning was fine and cool with the promise of a hot day ahead, but we had done our hills and we had a good track to walk. So with lighter packs and well pleased we set off. Away from the big hills we were on open moorland with the hot sun on us. Before we began to suffer the heat we reached the welcome shade of forestry, our walk was almost over. When we reached the car we found a note from the boys attached to the windscreen. They had got back to their tents late and well knackered. They must have lain in long because according to their note they had left for home a mere half an hour before us.

'See efter Skye . . .'

BY THE MONTH OF MAY I had been building a half-ton yacht with Bill McKay for his boss Ivor (who was the owner of *Linn Hi–Fi*) when suddenly our holiday came upon us. At this time I had six-teen Munros still to climb, and Rab had twelve. I had rented a house at Hungladder – near Kilmuir in the north-west side of the Trotternish peninsula – for three weeks for our family holiday. Rab Doyle and a pal of my son Peter were also coming. With Rab driving my car and with the loan of another from Ivor we set off to drive north. At Kyle of Lochalsh I was in front and drove straight onto the ferry without noticing that I had bypassed a large queue of cars in the car park waiting to board.

Kilmuir was situated not far from the Skye Folk Museum and quite near to where Flora MacDonald, of Bonnie Prince Charlie fame, is buried. But I had to return home almost as soon as I got there to help finish the boat. On my return to Skye a few days later I travelled up by bus. I recall having to change buses at Portree, and to pass the time I went into a small bar on the seafront. In front of everyone there the barman made a comment on my height – but when I gave him as good as he gave I was soon made most welcome. My arrival at Hungladder was also a warm one as the boys were glad to see their old man.

While I had been away Rab had been useful in driving the older boys around to spy out the sights. They had been birdwatching along the sea cliffs and had discovered an eagle's eyrie overlook-ing a nearby loch. I found it amusing months later watching a TV programme about eagles: the presenter was talking about this secret location where we had spent days watching the very same birds. After a few days being the good Dad, visiting castles and beaches, I set off with Rab on a bright Sunday morning to make our first climb in the Cuillin hills.

An early start saw us drive down the peninsula through Portree and on to park near the Sligachan Hotel. This was to become a routine drive on our visit to Skye. The mountain for the day was Sgurr nan Gillean by the so-called 'tourist route'. Leaving the hotel by the Carbost road we followed the path to the power house. Before us was the outline of our hill, with Am Basteir and the jagged Basteir Tooth clear and fearsome-looking. Crossing the burn we followed its meanderings across the moor, with our peak directly in front.

On reaching the Alt Dearg Beag we followed it for a short distance till we reached a marker cairn. Here we crossed the burn and turning left made for a dip on the right-hand side of the Nead na h'Iolaire. This part of the way was not well marked but on reaching the cairn overlooking Coire Riabhaid the path becomes clearer and is more so once clear of the corrie.

From now on the hard graft began. Plenty of cairns marked the way as it

Looking from Collies Edge to the Inn Pin

twisted in and out of a wilderness of boulders and scree below the Pinnacle Ridge. Ahead towered the shattered and almost horizontal skyline of the south-east ridge. We slowly scrambled up steep scree to eventually reach the cairn at its crest. Here we had a breather before making the final climb. When we set off again the going was rough but the climbing easy. We kept to the left side of the crest which looks into Lotta Corrie. A few cairns marked the route here until the ridge began to steepen. This is when we began to appreciate the adhesive properties of the black gabbro, the rock that the Cuillins are made of. We had been warned about this adhesion and the roughness of this rock and were told to take our old boots with us. By the time we went home I had worn out the toes of my boots as well as the seat of my trousers and my fingertips.

As we proceeded ever upwards we had to make liberal use of our hands to ensure safe progress. Near the top we swung to the right and encountered what the guidebook describes as a short hiatus which you have to step over boldly. I did so, concentrating on the summit and trying not to look down. Suddenly we were there on the tiny summit platform with its small cairn. Because the last hundred feet or so are so steep, the summit platform has a feeling of airy isolation. This is because as you sit at the cairn no part of the supporting ridges can be seen. While we sat drinking in the view there were a few people coming and going. One well-spoken old chap we got talking to was a member of the Alpine climbing club. After sharing my large flask of tea he suggested forming a Glasgow Scottish Alpine branch. From the summit of Gillean we had a bird's-eye view to the north of Pinnacle Ridge. We could see Knight's Peak, the fourth pinnacle. This is the key for those making the traverse of the whole ridge.

After a few photographs Rab as usual wanted to continue along to the next peak, but I was having none of this. The steepness of the ridge was bad enough but there was also the problem of getting past what was known as the 'Gendarme', or 'Policeman', a sensationally poised obelisk which is the crux to the descent to the Bealach a'Basteir. An obstacle not far along but barring progress to those of us who were not rock climbers – especially me, with no real head for heights. Not long after we left Skye the Gendarme succumbed to the effects of erosion and fell off the ridge. We returned the way we had come up. Going down was as difficult as the climb, not just because of the exposure near the top but because of the number of climbers on their way up. As we descended we could see a helicopter nearby. Later we found out that a woman had been killed on the ridge and two others injured so I felt quite happy that we had not been too ambitious that first day on these hills.

For the next two days the weather was dull and wet. We spent this time with May and the boys in shopping trips to Uig and Portree and visits to the nearby Skye Folk Museum. We took them walks around the nearby lochs and cliffs, looking at the sea birds and watching the eagles with their young.

By Wednesday we were off to the hills again. This time the plan was to climb the easiest peak in the Cuillins, Bruach na Frithe. A late start saw us drive to Sligachan again. The weather was initially bright but the forecast was for rain later. The ascent of this peak was just a long trudge with no real difficulties. As we climbed we soon found ourselves enclosed in swirling mist which blew eerily around the tops. Along with Bruach na Frithe we took in a top and decided to make an attempt on nearby Am Basteir, thinking that with the mist the drops would not be as intimidating. So on we went, following others up the ridge. Eventually we came to a place where we could see it was not the summit but just a drop in the ridge – but with the mist we could not see how much. Not wanting to give in we tried dropping down to get round but the hillside just dropped steeply into the mist. At one stage I was hanging on with my fingers and trying to feel the rock below with my feet. It might have only been inches or much more but there was no way I could tell.

As we sat pondering on what to do, a strapping young English girl appeared out of the mist with a rope wrapped around her shoulders and the backside ripped out of her breeches. She asked us what the problem was and when Rab told her that I could not reach the ridge below she simply grabbed me by the scruff of the neck and hoisted me straight onto the hidden ledge below. I was just too gobsmacked to say anything as she disappeared into the mist leaving us to struggle on behind. When we did reach the top the mist only cleared for a few minutes to let us see other jagged peaks sticking up out of a grey sea. Our way off the hill as usual was to retrace our steps. It was a damp and tired pair who made their way down that day and into the Sligachan for a welcome pint before heading back to the farmhouse.

Two days later we set off in very wet and misty conditions to climb Blaven, but we made a mess of navigating onto the hill. Thoroughly soaked, we decided to abort the climb for the day and instead went for a drive away down to the village of Elgol. As usual once away from the hills the weather cleared and a short walk along the shore gave us grand views of the misty Cuillins overlooking Loch Scavaig. The next day was a bit better weather-wise so we again drove down to Blaven. This time we had no trouble in finding our way onto the hill. However, the summit was shrouded in mist and we climbed the Munro and its top without seeing a view. By now I was down to thirteen Munros and Rab was at nine. That night we took the family up to the ruin of the castle at Duntulm. On the shore we found fossils and later went back around the road below the Quiraing and Staffin.

The next morning was a stunner as we drove to Glen Brittle to meet up with the Gleniffer, only to find that they had left without waiting for us. So off we went to climb ourselves. By now getting used to the tough terrain on these hills, we spent a long, hard day in which we climbed three Munros and two tops. It was only later in the day that we met up with the boys on Sgurr a Mhadhaidh. They were doing the same as us but in the opposite direction. Wee Jimmy warned us that we would need a rope on part of the ridge called the An Dorus gap. However, we could not be bothered burdening ourselves carrying a rope and soon parted, arranging to meet next day in the hostel. As we pushed on along the ridge we eventually came to this gap, which we passed by with little difficulty. Either we were getting used to the terrain by now or the boys were not.

We found that relentless days on these hills wore everyone down. Everyone at some time or another would sit down wrecked with their nerve gone. Sometimes it would happen on a relatively easy part of the ridge. As Rab and I drove into Glen Brittle to meet the boys we were a bit more apprehensive. Ken Lacy, the wee bloke who trained us to abseil at the Whangie, was here to see us climb the Inaccessible Pinnacle. The 'Inn Pin' has been the downfall of many would-be Munroists. It is a flake of rock sitting at the top of Sgurr Dhearg. The usual way up is to climb up, and at times astride, this flake of rock and to abseil down a mere sixty feet or so onto the mountain proper. The only problem is that there are sheer drops down each side of the mountain. As we all set off the weather was not good: it began to rain heavily and was quite windy on the tops. Buoyed up by adrenaline we were all soon standing at the bottom of the Pin. Most of the group were reluctant to climb in such weather; I didn't relish climbing with waterproofs on. The only good thing was that there were no views to put you off. So it was Rab Doyle and Stukky Alexander who made the climb that day on the Pin, with Ken leading. For the rest of us, it was a frustrated group who came off the hill that night, psyched up and extremely tetchy.

The next morning after we met up and passed round the ropes and gear I climbed the hill in record time. This time I was going for the top or bust. Although dry it was misty on the tops. As far as I was concerned this was a good thing. The last thing I wanted was to experience the exposure on the Pin. Jimmy and myself went up first, with Ken leading. I was in the middle and would be anchor man for Jimmy. Ken started off up and soon all that I could see from the bottom of the climb was the ropes disappearing into the mist. When he was ready Ken called for me to come and up I went. I was climbing quickly and quite boldly. At first I was on one side of the flake and suddenly I felt that, like a cartoon character, I was climbing in mid-air.

As I got to Ken I anchored myself and called Jimmy on up. Here, halfway up the Pin, as I wound the slack of the rope I had time to ponder where I was. As Jimmy came up to me the mist suddenly parted to reveal breathtaking drops all around us from our lofty position. All I could say was, 'Jimmy, whitever the fuck ye dae, don't look doon!' Quickly we moved over the top and to the cheers of the others sitting on the ridge below we prepared to abseil off the short side of the pinnacle. This was done in good style and Jimmy and myself took our place on the ridge while the last two, Chris and Jackie, made ready to go up. As they nervously roped up Rab was psyching them up like a boxing trainer giving instructions to the guy in the ring – especially Jackie whose legs were shaking. Rab said that there was a good hand hold halfway up at a particular part of the climb. As they climbed one

at a time up the rock with rope trailing behind them to disappear in the mist we could hear Jack shout, 'Ah cannae find the hold!' As they eventually appeared on the summit we could hear him shouting, 'Ah've loast the key tae ma arse, an ah'm shiteing through ma teeth!' When they had abseiled off and we had all regrouped we posed for photographs in front of the Pinnacle. We were now confident that we would all finish our Munros, sometime. With the Pin behind us we were on a roll. Rab had only four to do. So we drove to the

Peter abseiling off the Inn Pin

hostel to meet the boys. They were doing other hills that day so Rab and I were off to Sgurr Mhic Choinnich and Sgurr Alasdair. For us, this turned out a hot sunny day with stunning walks into the deep Coire Laggan. We drove ourselves up relentless scree slopes on bare waterless hills. Mhic Choinnich was like sitting astride a huge church roof. We could see all of the Cuillins and the surrounding islands of Rhum and Eigg. The only hills that had cloud on their tops were those that the others were climbing on.

Not being rock climbers we retraced our steps from the airy summit of Mhic Choinnich. About halfway along we turned off the summit ridge and onto a narrow ledge which slants at an angle towards the bealach of our next hill. This is known as Collie's Ledge after the well-known climber Norman Collie. Once on the bealach we could soon look up the climbers' route along the ridge An Thearlaich.

Our next summit for the day now was Sgurr Alasdair. The route up was by way of the famous 'stone shoot'. This is a huge gash in the side of the mountain running from top to bottom at a steep angle. Many years ago it was possible to run down the scree in this but now all the loose scree is at the bottom leaving large rough rocks to clamber up and down. When we had struggled up the stone shoot, now in the welcome shade, we found ourselves on a bealach with a short climb up to the summit of Sgurr Alasdair. Again Rab wanted to go off along the ridge but I insisted on going back down the way we had come up.

The descent from Alasdair was long and weary. In the corrie we were in the full heat of a baking sun as we picked our way down through the hot bare rocks. As Rab looked likely to complete his Munros the next day he decided to call in at the Sligachan hotel to purchase a bottle of the local whisky. It had become a tradition that when someone was finishing the Munros they bought a bottle of the local brand of the watter of life. So for Rab it was a bottle of Talisker to celebrate the coming day.

For our last day on the Cuillins we were up and away early, roaring down the by now familiar road to Sligachan. At the hostel we teamed up with the boys and on another hot sunny morning we made our last foray into the hills. Our route lay up through Coire Grundha where we soon began to feel the effect of a blazing sun. Our hills for the day were the two Munros at the end of the Cuillin Ridge – Sgoran Dhubh Mhor and Sgoran Dhubh Beag, more commonly called the Dubbs. Our progress over these two hills was slow, not just because of the heat: although not as narrow-ridged they were probably the roughest of the Skye hills. At times I had to be pushed and lifted up on some of the rough parts that I could not reach. At last we were all gathered on the final cairn and stood waiting for Rab to ascend to the cairn. With a triumphant flourish he swept up onto the

cairn brandishing his Talisker and wearing his white silk scarf. We all sat around the cairn supping our Talisker with the isle of Rum before us and behind all of the Cuillins basking in the warm sun. There was one more lesser top on the ridge to take in as we haphazardly made our way down to sea level. Every so often we had a stop for more Talisker and where

Smiles all round after conquering the Pin

there was water to put in it, it was the same colour as the whisky. By the time we got to sea level we were all falling around in the bogs and were liberally covered in peat. The Skye Munros now behind, I had only five more to climb. They had been tough going for everyone, emotionally and physically. On a later harrowing trip to these hills George McCall summed them up, as he sat in the Carbost Inn with a large cigar in one hand and a large whisky in the other. With a smug and relieved grin he mused, 'See efter Skye, evrythin else is a' shite!'

The Last Munro, May 1989

ON 20 MAY 1989 I FINALLY finished my Munros, on Aonach Mhor. This was the culmination of many years on the Munro-bagging treadmill. The event was attended by most of the Glennifer team as well as wee Billy Billings. In a small convoy of cars we drove to the wee car park at the end of Glen Nevis. From here we made our way up into the upper part of the glen through the narrow gorge, emerging into the wide flat meadows just before Steal. The gorge was as usual a spectacular scene with its strange pot holes carved by water action. We spent some time on the wire bridge near Steal posing for photos with the tumbling waterfall beyond. We remembered the first time we had crossed the bridge when there were only two wire strands to hold on to rather than three. Just beyond Steal we turned up into the col between Aonach Mhor and Carn Mhor Dhearg. There was a mad flurry as the party split up with small groups shooting off in different directions. It was not unusual in the later stages of doing our Munros to find everyone climbing different hills. For some of the team it was a necessity because the limits of age and fitness were fast catching up with them.

When the main group reached the bealach between Aonach Mhor and Carn Mhor Dhearg we split up again. Rab, Chris and I turned off to ascend Carn Mhor Dhearg in the thickening mist, while the others set off up Aonach Mhor to meet up with us later. When we reached the top of Carn Mhor Dhearg with the mist swirling about us I was feeling very elated now that there was only one more to go. When I think about it now I wonder why I did the two that day. Why did we punish ourselves when another shorter day out would have seen only one hill to climb?

As we descended to the bealach and began the ascent of my last Munro the day began to improve. Once on the long, rounded ridge we ambled along to the summit. An RAF mountain rescue team that had been on exercise in the area joined in our celebration.

As the boys sat in the sun basking in my glory Bob Alexander was listening through earphones to a vital Old Firm game on the radio. Every now and then he would let out a mad roar as if a goal had been scored. This upset Chris, who supported the opposite side, but later Bob confessed that it was all bluff.

On the hill that day we had no drink that I remember but we made up for that back at our campsite at Glen Nevis. Big Al had his new 'space tent' which seemed to hold all of us. For me, exact details of that night are, to say the least, sketchy. I was as drunk as a skunk. More than a few of us were to be seen clutching a bottle of malt whisky to our breast. Billy was well steaming, doing what he does best – kicking over everyone's drinks. Chris lay in a corner, his eyes rolling around as if on gimbals. Bob Alexander, like me, was tenderly nursing a bottle of malt and gibbering to

Celebrations at Glen Nevis campsite

himself. We sang songs and made a lot of noise. I vaguely remember hearing some nearby camper asking us in a rather posh voice to be quiet. 'I say, cheps, would you please keep the jolly old noise down, what?' We replied asking if he would care to partake in a wee bevvy: 'Haw, hey, dae ye waant a wee swally, china?' When his reply was in the negative we promptly told him to 'shut up' and 'fuck off'. When I eventually passed out I was trussed up into my sleeping bag and left to drift off into the oblivious state that the Munroist deserves. Just before I checked out, the last thing I remember was them laughing at me: Rab's drunken sunburnt bawface and George the 'Preesident', fu' as a wulk.

Inevitably the next day dawned. Someone presented me with an unwelcome plateful of breakfast: eggs, bacon, sausage. This was a drastic way to determine my powers of recovery. Could I at least swallow some of it? No, just looking at it prompted me to throw up. Unable to stand upright, I crawled to the nearby toilets, hanging on to the short grass, scared that I would spin off into space if I let go. When I reached the toilets I was unable to decide whether to sit on the seat or put my head down the pan – at times both were necessary. The last time I was this ill was the first night at sea with old McKay on our trip to Lymington. For most of the day Rab and Billy attempted to sober me up enough to drive home. The rest of the boys had already gone. It was late that day that we left. I had finished the Munros, but I would be climbing many of them again.

Whiteout

ON SUNDAY 1 APRIL, TWO fools left Yoker and drove north to Gerry Howkins' hostel at Achnashellach in Strathcarron. The last time we had been in this area was when we climbed the Torridon mountains with the Gleniffer boys in September 1986. We had not come to climb hills but to do what we called 'link-up' walks that would connect previous exploits on the big hills. After booking in at Gerry's we drove along to Achnashellach station where there lived an old couple called Donald and Dolly. Rab had met them on a previous visit, and we wanted to ask if we could leave the car near the station for a couple of days. So next morning we left Gerry's and parked the car in an old open shed that might at one time have garaged coaches. As I backed into it, the rear wheels sank into thick, gooey mud. Well, we would deal with that when we returned – for now we were off to the hills.

We caught the train and travelled the four miles or so down the glen to Strathcarron. Now we could begin our walk proper. Crossing the road we turned up towards the farm at Tulloch towards the Bealach a'Ghlas-chnoic that lies between Glas Bheinn 711 metres and Torr na h-Iolaire. We were walking on a good track and made good time. Soon we were over the bealach and dropping down again. Before us we could see a small loch, Loch Coultrie. Beyond it runs the road from Strathcarron through Glen Sheildaig to Torridon. At a place named Ceann-loch-damh we crossed a bridge and began to walk along the shore of Loch Damh. We were once more away from roads and strolling along a good level path beside a wild highland loch. About three miles long, the loch sits between Beinn Damh (901 metres) on one side and Ben Shieldaig (439 metres) on the other. On reaching the north end of the loch the track turns away and comes out on the motor road at Loch Torridon. Here we swung right and walked the three miles along it to the youth hostel at Torridon. The hostel was fairly quiet when we booked in for the one night, unlike the last time we were there en masse with the heavy team.

We awoke next morning to a white landscape. During the night it had snowed and all the surrounding peaks were well covered in snow. This we had not bargained for. We were now on the wrong side of the mountains. By road Achnashellach was miles away and we had no choice but to stick to the original plan and cross over through the hills back to where we had started from.

Leaving the hostel, we only walked a short distance to the bridge over the River Torridon before pushing straight into the

Fionn bothy

hills on a fairly good path that led us quickly up, contouring at times along beside a jumble of small lochans. Near the largest of these we found the path difficult to follow in deepening snow. As we pulled up to the top of the bealach which lies below Meall Dearg and the Munro of Maol Chean-dearg (the scene of previous adventures), it began to snow heavily. Struggling drunkenly on, we found it impossible to navigate. I could not see the compass at one point – I had spindrift blown into my eyes. We could only stagger on hoping that we were nearly over the summit of the path. Falling about under the weight of our packs and buffeted by the driving wind and snow, we were slowly weakening. If this kept up we would soon be in real trouble.

Suddenly the snow began to ease and we could see more of the landscape around us. We thought we were now over the hump, but as the sunlight shone on distant hills we realised that we had turned to the north-east and were looking back into Glen Torridon and at the mountains of Liathach and Beinn Eighe. We had no option but to turn back up the path for three quarters of a mile to gain the right way off. We followed our own footprints then turned down into the correct glen.

The day turned to showers with sunny spells and as we passed below Maol Chen-dearg we gazed in awe at the gully, outlined by snow, which we had climbed with wee Stukky in 1984. Our path now led us past Loch Coire Fionnaraich and down to the Fionn Choire bothy we had stopped at before. The bothy by this time was in a poor condition: much of the wooden panelling had gone and there was no upstairs. All that was left was a bare room with an old table, a couple of chairs and a fireplace filled with rubbish. However, we were grateful to find ourselves inside, out of the elements. We stripped off our wet gear and had a drum-up.

We now set off to walk out to the main road a couple of miles away at Coulags. As we had walked this stretch before we tried harder for a lift. Our luck was in – along the road came a huge furniture van. We were told to jump in the back and were hoping that we could lie back in comfort on somebody's seats. Instead we found ourselves inside an empty van. As he took off along the winding road we had to hang on to straps for dear life as we were thrown about like sacks of potatoes. Luckily we only had a few miles to go and were dropped off at Achnashellach before I was seasick. After thanking Donald and Dolly for letting us park the car we eventually extricated the thing from the muddy shed and headed south for hame.

When Wan Door Closes

SOMEONE ONCE SAID THAT the finest sight for any Scotsman was the high road to England. For me, the opposite became true. In the spring of 1991, at what proved to be the peak of my yacht-building career, I returned from working on the south coast. I had been to a personal hell and back in a very short space of time. It began nearly two years before with a chance phone call from the south coast of England. I was at Ratagan youth hostel with the boys at a time when work had been scarce. From out of the blue I was offered work at a custom yacht builders in Hampshire. After a hectic day or so two of us were heading south to an uncertain future.

Far from home for months at a time, we ate, slept and worked till we dropped. Twelve hours a day, seven days a week. The money was great. We were at the top; we could do no wrong. However, very slowly the cracks began to appear – a crushing, abject loneliness that seemed to strike worse at night in cold dreary digs with your loved ones far away. Immersing ourselves in work was the only way to keep such thoughts from our minds. Imperceptibly the work tempo began to slow, as exhaustion and fatigue took its toll. It began with the odd night off to relax in the local pub, but soon we were drinking more and more. As Christmas time approached we all became excited by the prospect of going home to our families and when the time came it seemed that the whole of the south coast was on the move. All of us migrant workers scattered in every direction in a mass exodus.

We were always nervous of travelling home. It seemed that every time we migrated north or south there was some disaster or another. On a previous trip we had been in the south at the time of the Piper Alpha tragedy and on the way home by train we passed near Bradford at the same time as the terrible football ground fire. The next time we changed our plans at the last minute to come home by train: it was the day of the Clapham rail crash. Worse was to follow. Coming home we passed close to the Midlands air crash across the M1 motorway. We began to feel as if at some point we might become involved in some terrible catastrophe. On a dismal December day we left Southampton laden down with Christmas presents and set off on the long drive north. As usual on a long drive we played tapes and never thought of listening to the radio. We had no way of knowing that anything was amiss till we arrived near the sleepy Borders town of Lockerbie. The traffic heading north came to a complete standstill: ahead the sky was lit by a glowing orange light. Confusion reigned – lorry drivers spoke of IRA bombs and of an explosion at a petrol station, but no one knew what had happened. Eventually the police began to sort the traffic out but after a long drive I did not relish a detour almost to the Ayrshire coast. Instead we fell in behind a lorry that was headed for Whiteinch in Glasgow, not far from my home. We followed him as he swung away east of Lockerbie through the deserted towns of Selkirk, Langholm and Kelso. But finally even he gave up and pulled off the road for the night. I had little choice but to drive on, through a horrible night with near horizontal rain battering us across the winding Borders roads. Somehow I got back on to the main route north at Moffat and arrived in Yoker just before dawn – my wife frantic with worry and us totally unaware of the terrible truth of the previous evening, that a plane had been bombed out of the sky.

It was not easy to make the return journey south that New Year. In due course the hectic pace and harsh demands of our work caught up with us. On what turned out to be my last project we had as usual begun the job full of good intentions: our feeling that we were the best still carried us along. Right at the start of this new boat we were building it all began to fall apart. I was lofting out the shape of the hull and deck but I had unknowingly made a serious mistake with some of the dimensions of the deck. The construction progressed at a rapid pace and we were also working on another yacht at the same time. When the day came to join hull and deck together, the cockpit flooring of the deck was found to be completely the wrong size and shape. For me this was a major disaster and effectively the end of my yacht-building career. That night I returned to my lodgings and began to drink myself senseless. Of the next few days I remember little, only that I never went back to the job. The other Scots boys sharing my digs kept away from me: they offered no support and just left me to it. After a while I realised I was not wanted. I packed all my things into my car and moved out. I went on a massive bender. I just left the car lying with my tools and clothes in a quiet lane near the village of Pennington. For a few days I lived rough in the nearby New Forest, wandering about wondering what to do. Sleeping rough was no real hardship after years of going to the hills.

Custom yachtbuilder

I eventually gravitated to Southampton and found myself on the streets. This was the worst time I have ever experienced. Much of the time I was drunk, dirty, and by now totally out of my mind. I had reached the bottom in a very short space of time. I slept in doorways, underpasses, anywhere I could get out of the weather. Soon I was begging for money on the streets. It was only a matter of time before the inevitable happened. One night I was arrested for causing a disturbance and thrown into the cells for the night. It was there I was recognised by someone who knew me – a fellow Scot who had troubles of his own. He took me under his wing and did his best to sort me out. With some help from this friend I returned home to Glasgow.

No one who knew me in Glasgow ever knew what had happened. Most people just thought that the job had simply came to an end. Well, the job had ended but so had my days as a yacht builder. For a long time afterwards I was out of work and suffering depression. Many a time I found myself suffering black moods of self-doubt standing beside the oily waters of the Clyde trying to convince myself that life was worth living and that suicide was too easy an option. My energy for life had taken a big knock and it would take me a long time to get my life together again. There were still plenty of knockdowns but, after all, a Govan man just gets up and carries on. Slowly I began going out on the hills again. Yet with the drawing power of the Munros well behind us it was difficult to feel the old enthusiasm and challenge. What I needed was a purpose to keep going to the hills. Many others I knew had simply disappeared once they had completed their Munros – this was not what I had wanted. I had yet to discover the lure of the Corbetts. About this time I wrote to HF Holidays to enquire about becoming an HF leader. I was invited to attend a course at Coniston in the Lake District where indeed I became an HF walks leader. Sometimes I am convinced that I was only picked as a token Scot, but in the next few years I took several thousand people to the hills.

Bob Alexander's Last Munro

IN THE DARK AND DESERTED early hours Rab Doyle and I met at the corner of my street. This was the first I had seen of the old yin in almost two years. We had both gone our own ways for a time. Rab had just disappeared from the climbing scene and during that time he had lost his youngest daughter. We had little to say to one another as we stood waiting to be picked up by the Gleniffer team who were off to the island of Mull. We had been invited to join them to celebrate Bob Alexander's last Munro, Ben More. They arrived in a large orange Ford Transit minibus. This strange vehicle belonged to Chris (the handsome fool): it was powered by petrol but with the flick of a switch it could run on bottled gas. This I had never seen before – to Rab and I it elevated the suspicion that Paisley men are frugally challenged to new and unheard-of heights. With the usual Paisley planning we did not head up the A82 towards Crianlarich: a longish route but a good road. No, we went up the 'Rest' and over by Inveraray – shorter in miles but slower and extremely winding. All the ingredients for a good spew, not helped by Jackie Harrison and George the Preesident puffing away on cigarettes and cigars.

All the gang were there – me, Rab Doyle, George McCall, Bob Alexander, Big Al, Wee Jimmy Galloper, Hughie Hart, Andy Murdoch, Chris Barclay, plus a few others. At Oban we boarded the ferry for a good crossing to Mull. From Craignure we drove across the island to make camp on the shore at the foot of the hill. Once this was done we were allocated drinks to carry up onto the hill. Instead of climbing directly up to Ben More we were going to climb the whole of the mountain, taking in the smaller peak and the ridge to the main summit. It was only when we reached the snow line that we realised we could have a difficult time. The hill was not only clad in snow – which we had not expected – but was covered in ice as well. The last thing we wanted, with all our 'experience' and carrying rucksacks full of strong drink, was to have to call out mountain rescue.

But all was well. On the summit of Ben More we duly toasted Bobby's last Munro with the usual reverence and ceremony that the occasion deserved. Flourishing a bottle of Ben More whisky as tradition demands, Bobby went round filling glasses till the bottle was dead. As per usual on a last Munro event I don't remember much about the descent, and I don't suppose many of the others do either. Suffice to say that the evening was spent with all of us crammed inside the minibus, singing and drinking. Hughie Hart kept going outside but he would forget about the step and spent much of the night lying outside on the grass face down. At some point the evening's festivities must have come to an end and those unworthy of a bunk in the bus had to crawl into the various tents. Next morning we all drove into Tobermory for a walk about and an attempt to sober up before the long journey home. Bobby Alexander's was one of the few overnight last-Munro trips the boys made; any others were day trips – not nearly as much fun.

Midnight on the Mamores

TO COMPLETE A MIDNIGHT traverse of the whole Glen Nevis area was a dream I had nurtured for many years. I had read of the late Philip Tranter's exploits on these hills and even of a lady in her sixties who had completed the round in something like twenty-four hours. On a splendid summer's evening I found myself in the company of two old climbing friends, Bob Alexander and Derek Sakol, on a leisurely drive up to the HF guest house at Loch Leven. Here we enjoyed a pint of Guinness before heading round to start our walk at Glen Nevis hostel. Part of the plan was to set off quite late and to walk by the light of the moon and torches. Our first hill was Mullach nan Coirean. To reach it we walked along the Glen Nevis road to Polldubh where we turned off, up and into the forest. The path through the trees soon emerged in a corrie where we decided to turn right and strike for the ridge proper. On a fine evening with a glorious sunset we wended our way through broken rocks to the summit, where we arrived at ten.

From Mullach the ridge wanders east towards Stob Ban, our next hill. As we traversed along we could see the lights of Fort William on our left and the lights of Ballachulish below to the south. In the far distance the lights of Kinlochleven beckoned us onward. About halfway to Stob Ban the light began to go, and instead of us walking by the light of the moon it began to cloud over till we were in complete darkness, tracing our route by torchlight. At the stroke of midnight we stood on the summit of Stob Ban. The feeble beams of torches were lost in the inky dark when we shone them from the ridge and it was with great difficulty that we slowly made our way down to the next col. Bob, Derek and myself were all doing quite well: providing the weather held we were confident of completing the round. Upon reaching the col we followed the path along to the small lochan lying below the next summit, and here we decided to rest till dawn.

As we were carrying neither tent nor sleeping bags we simply lay down fully clothed with space blankets and bivvy bags and tried to get some sleep. Around about five, frozen and with chattering teeth, we awoke in the pre-dawn light and made ourselves a hot drink. Too cold to linger, we were soon on our way once more. Instead of going up onto the next Munro, Sgurr An Iubhair, we climbed a well-worn track from the lochan to the ridge which runs out to the big Munro of Sgurr a'Mhaim. Here we left our packs. This is a fairly narrow ridge, only a foot wide in places, and is known as the Devil's Ridge. About halfway along there is a gap which can be crossed by taking a long jump at it, but the faint-hearted can simply drop off onto the side of the ridge and pass it by. Beyond this point the ridge widens and climbs steeply up to the summit of Sgurr a'Mhaim. This we duly reached in good time.

Many years before, this fine peak (which is seen at its best from lower Glen Nevis) was nearly the death of myself and John Cuthill the first time we climbed it. Unlike many trips which ended in Fort William High Street we had actually got on to these hills. John and I had left his trusty Hillman Imp at Polldubh and set off up the glen on a grey forbidding day in early spring with low cloud and the tops well covered in snow. Having climbed up to the col and being new to this hill we veered off the ridge in thickening mist and soon found ourselves on steepening ground in deep, soft snow that reached above our knees. A strange thing about being in thick mist on any mountain is the feeling of being cut off from everything. Nothing else matters except the small immediate area within your limited visibility. The place where we now found ourselves, out of the wind, was totally silent. The only noise was made by us as we sweated and thrashed painfully upwards. It wasn't even cold and if we had been a bit more experienced this would have alerted us to danger. We were unwittingly trying to cross a slope liable to avalanche at any moment. We were in a large hollow. John was about halfway across the steep slope and I was about follow. We had stopped to catch our breath when from above and between us snow started to trickle down the incline. As we looked up to see where it was coming from we were shocked to see a huge crack running right across the slope just above us. Gripped with fear, we froze, unable to advance or retreat, too scared to make any noise. Neither of us had an ice-axe or rope – for all the good they would do. John was the first to break the spell. Being nearest to the safer ground he signalled that he was moving, but very carefully. All I could do was follow his footsteps and pray very hard. As I eased myself on to a flat step with little snow the whole area behind us broke away – almost without a sound – and slipped down the mountain into the mist till we eventually heard a faraway rumble below us.

It was two shocked and badly rattled Munro-baggers who reached the cairn that day. Unsure of the best thing to do we had carried on to the summit without thinking what was the safest way off the mountain. Still shaken, we looked at the map and decided to head in a south-easterly direction on what we thought was the best route down, thinking that once down we would simply follow the glen into Glen Nevis. However, as on many days, we found there was to be a sting in the tail. We did get off the hill but instead of an easy walk out we found ourselves standing at the top of a seemingly huge waterfall looking straight down to the wee building of Steall in Glen Nevis far below. Well, we learned a hard lesson that day as we came across the wire bridge at Steall, soaked to the skin after scrambling down by the waterfall. We had escaped an avalanche and badly misread our maps. And to finish it off, the wire bridge then had only two strands of wire instead of three.

I was thinking of that first trip to Sgurr a'Mhaim as we left the cairn early in the morning, with cloud and mist swirling slowly around the nearby summits, and retraced our way along the Devil's Ridge to where we had left our rucksacks. Our next top was Sgurr an Ubhair. A steep rocky path led us quickly to its summit. From here we had an easy descent to our next peak, Am Bodach, from which we came down what I always consider one of the trickiest parts of the Mamore hills. This descent, down a very steep and rough path onto the next top, has caused me problems a few times when leading inexperienced walkers – on one occasion a walker above me dislodged rocks and I had just happened to step off to the side of the track when a rock the size of a piano flew by me out of the mist. Our next top was reached over an easy up-and-down grassy part of the ridge. Here, at the summit of Stob Choire A'Charn, I suggested to the others that I

would wait here with their packs if they wanted to make an attempt on the twin Munros of An Gearanach and An Garbhanach that lie off the main ridge. This they were happy to do, so I settled down on the summit to wait for them. As they set off the mist began to roll in and soon they were out of sight. Despite

John Cuthill on Sgurr a'Mhaim

being unable to see them I could clearly hear them as they climbed out over the two hills.

After a while they both returned and we continued along the ridges to the rougher tops at the eastern end of the range. Na Gruagaichean was soon topped, but I could see that Bobby was tiring: we all were. I just thought at first that it must be the early start, with little or no sleep. Usually this wears off and you just stagger on. The next and, as it turned out, the last summit was that of Binnien Mhor, the highest of the Mamores. As we struggled up the hill the weather began to deteriorate quickly. By the time we reached the cairn on the top it was raining hard. Bobby was looking very weak; at times I thought he was going to collapse on me. The only thing to do was to continue towards the next hill but turn off at the col and then drop down into Glen Nevis. This we duly did but all thoughts of doing the complete traverse of the glen were now off. It was obvious that Bob's fitness was not what it should have been for such a hard trip.

Somehow we made our way down into the glen. The rain was continuous and very cold. We had not been prepared for such cold conditions at this time of year. Wading the river we gained the path and slowly made our way along towards the Nevis gorge beyond Steall's wire bridge and the tumbling waterfall. At the wee car park I just lay on my back in the middle of the road, oblivious to the rain. We still had to walk down the glen to the hostel where the cars were parked, along a hard tarmac road. At that moment a car drew in to turn around. With quick thinking, wee Bobby pushed Derek towards the door and asked the driver to run him down the glen. As Derek got in and was driven off we just flopped down again. About twenty minutes later Derek returned with his car to pick us up, thus ending our only attempt to do the round of Glen Nevis. We had been beaten not only by the weather but also by our lack of fitness.

Assynt

EASTER. THE PROMISE OF spring, another year with new hills to conquer and the start of the youth hostels opening. Rab Doyle had finally been persuaded to return once more to the hills, after his self-enforced retirement, by his old pal Billy Billings and myself. Billy Billings had been a walker from way back but for forty years or so he never went near the hills. He made an attempt to climb the Munros but had left it much too late. It was once said that if there was a hole to fall down or a rock to trip over Billy would find it. A hapless climber, he was in his day described by his peers as a hard road walker. With his distinctive gait, Billy had been known to walk many of his contemporaries into the ground. Just like wee Stukky he was a product of the thirties and had been part of the pre-war outdoor revolution. Rab and myself were taken aback when he told us quite out of the blue that he used to spend weekends at the famous fire at Craigallion and that he knew people like Jock Nimlin, Nimmo, Saunders and others who passed into the folklore of the outdoors at that time. Billy was probably well known around the fire: he would have made the tea and more than likely would have tripped over the same tea cans and put the fire out. However, to give Billy his due he was there and in his day must have done some hard walking in his own right. In 1932 at the age of sixteen, Billy and a friend – at twenty-one regarded as older and wiser – set off one Saturday after their work. This was not unusual: many guys worked Saturday mornings then went to the hills. Billy and his pal set off from Clydebank walking up Kilbowie road, then almost a country lane, with eight sandwiches in their pockets. Mainly on roads they walked towards Aberfoyle before turning west in the direction of Ben Lomond. With their pieces long eaten and night upon them, Billy's pal must have realised that it would be a cold night and that they needed shelter. Coming upon a lonely farm they knocked on the door and asked the wee boy who answered it to ask his father if they could doss in a nearby outhouse. Securing permission, they settled down in hay and at least under a roof, and before they turned in the man of the house told them to come in for breakfast next morning.

Wee Billy had for ages kept winding us up with three trips he had done just after the war: an outing to the Cairngorms; a climb on An Teallach; and a trip to Lochinver. What was so extraordinary about these trips was that the little bugger had an amazing collection of old black and white photographs. It was a case of, 'Oh, ye should see An Challach' or, 'Ye should see ra Shelter Stone.' One at a time we made our own trips to these places and after each one he never mentioned them again. So this was why we were headed for Assynt up in the far north-west. A run of a good four and a half hours up the A9 took us over the Kessock bridge and on to our destination which was the youth hostel at 'Carbisdoyle Castle' or 'Rabby Doyle's Castle'. This was the first weekend that the hostels were open for the season, but we were surprised to find the place was busy with foreign tourists. However, the castle is enormous with plenty of room for everyone. In the evening Billy-boy entertained the guests by performing his acrobatic tricks in the common room. Next morning after our hostel chores we collected our cards and set off, heading west along Glen Oykell.

As we drove on, the western horizon soon filled with snow-clad mountains. At Ledmore Junction we stopped to take some photos. Ledmore Junction must be one of the most misnamed places in the Highlands. A few years previously wee Jimmy Gallagher, while touring in the area, saw it on the maps and being short of supplies thought this would be a place to stock up on food. Unfortunately there is nothing here except two lonely roads meeting in the middle of nowhere. Turning north we drove on by Inchnadamph and then along the shores of Loch Assynt. Finally we drove into the busy fishing port of Lochinver. Here we parked the car and set off to walk the four miles or so into the bothy of Suileag or, as we called it, 'Sealegs'.

Carrying full packs along a fairly easy path we finally reached the bothy which sits just about one hundred yards off the path. We found the place empty and fairly tidy. Across the glen rose the bulk of Suilven with its odd rounded shape. It was still quite early in the day so we found some shovels and set about cutting some peat on the hillside behind the bothy. That evening we had a merry time with a good fire and, to round off our meal, a wee dram of Talisker whisky.

Although it was very windy during the night we awoke to a fine day and prepared our breakfast before setting out for our hill –

Peter on the summit of Canisp

not Suilven but Canisp lying to the east of us. The terrain here is a mass of small hillocks, and as Billy was going at his usual slow speed we lost sight of him very quickly. We waited on the path for ages wondering where the hell he was. Finally we decided to carry on without him, determined not to let him ruin the walk. Ascending steadily, we were soon rewarded with the most spectacular views of the surrounding hills all rising from a landscape of small lochans. To our right rose Suilven looking like an upturned ship, while to our left we could see the snow-covered peaks of Quinaig and away to the east the Munros of Ben More Assynt and Conival. On reaching the snowy summit we sat in the sun drinking in the views all round. If Billy had got lost, well, we would think about looking for him after we got our hill. We set off from the cairn at length to return the way we had come. About four hundred feet from the summit we came upon Billy making his way up the hill. Furious, Rab asked him where he had got to but, stubborn to the last, Billy would offer no explanation and would not turn back. Instead he was adamant about continuing up the hill. At this Rab got a map out and made him sign a declaration that we would not be responsible for his actions. None too pleased, we made our way down the hill and once on the track made good time back to the bothy.

As we prepared our evening meal we pondered on the wee man's stupidity. By now it had been dark for over an hour and a half. We had put a candle in the window – as the bothy lay off the path it would be possible for him to walk straight past. Eventually he appeared, totally unconcerned at the trouble he had caused, and simply proceeded to make his own dinner. This involved using all three stoves that we had and much waste of food he had not carried in. As the night wore on we drank some more whisky to make things a wee bit more bearable. The fire was not so good this time and as it was now too dark to bring in more peat we suddenly had an idea. The bothy had recently had a new roof put on it and there was a large wooden ladder lying in one of the rooms. Not wishing to be seen as vandals we tried to remove the ladder from the building. After spending quite some time trying to get it out of the door we eventually got the bow saw out, cut the ladder into pieces and sent it out of the building through the chimney.

The next morning saw Rab and I up early but Billy was only roused with great difficulty. He was renowned for his tardiness in the mornings. While breakfast was on we made ready to leave the bothy. As we were sweeping out some people arrived. It seemed that they were assessors for the Duke of Edinburgh's award scheme. Seemingly there were parties out all over the area and this lot were using Suileag bothy as a base for monitoring them. It was obvious that we were making them feel uncomfortable. And we suspected that they knew we were the culprits who had burnt the ladder. We now felt that it really was time to leave – except Billy, who as usual was messing about and getting nowhere. Eventually Rab cracked up. Grabbing Bill's old Bergen rucksack he began to stuff everything into it: clothes, food, sleeping bag, the lot. With a final flourish he stuck his boot in the bag and stuffed in what was left before grabbing Bilious by the scruff of the neck and bundling him out of the door. In order to confuse the people now gathering in the bothy we decided to split up: Rab and Bilious would walk out on the track north to the road at Little Assynt while I would exit the way we had walked in.

At Lochinver I picked up the car and drove round to pick the pair of them up, then continued round to the Inchnadamph Hotel where we had a pub lunch. With time on our hands we drove back into Lochinver and had a walk about the harbour till it was time to head for Achmelvich and book into the youth hostel. We had a quiet night there as the weather had turned grey and damp.

The next morning we left the hostel not to climb but to explore the coast to the west. On a day that would turn to mixed showers, windy but sunny and warm, we drove out on single-track roads as far as the lighthouse buildings at Cluas Deas point. From here we walked across a mixture of cliffs and moorland out to the point of Stoer. Standing on the cliffs we could look down on the sea stack of the Old Man of Stoer. You could see hanging from the top various pieces of slings and ropes left behind by climbers. On the way back to the hostel the car's oil warning light began to flash. Thinking that there was something serious I nursed it as far as I thought safe, then I started to walk back to Lochinver to find a garage. Fortunately I quickly obtained a lift both ways and having put some oil in the engine we were soon on our way back to the hostel.

Later that evening we all decided to walk the track from Achmelvich to Lochinver that had featured in Bill's photos of his trip forty years before – partly to lay this ghost of Billy's and partly to sample a Lochinver haddock supper. As we set off from the hostel it was quite light so we decided not to wear our boots or take waterproofs. The path turned out to be very muddy and soon our shoes were a real mess. However, we bashed on and soon arrived in the township. We made straight for the main hotel where we ordered up haddock teas, except Bill who turned his nose up at this and settled for a healthy meal of lasagne. His turned out to be rotten while Rab and myself enjoyed the best fish and chips we ever tasted. On emerging from the hotel to walk back we found that it was now raining . We had no choice but to plod back over the hill to the hostel, but at least we had been well fed and no more would we have to listen to Billy rant about Lochinver.

Our course was now set for home but at a leisurely pace. Leaving Achmelvich we drove south to Ullapool, stopping often for photos. There we topped up with petrol and had something to eat before continuing on our way. Leaving Loch Broom behind we turned off at Braemore Junction to have a look at the Corrieshalloch Gorge and the falls of Measach. This was a day in which we were just tourists. The falls were in good form: with lots of rain they were in full flow, the water dark brown with peat. While we were in this area we decided to go down the Destitution Road for a look at Fain bothy, our old campsite. The bothy was in as bad a condition as we remembered, but the views of An Teallach were as spectacular as ever. Returning to Braemore, we headed east along the Dirie Mhor road to the Altguish Inn, the scene of a previous campsite, and we stopped for a pint. From there we drove to our next tourist stop, the falls of Rogie. We were the only people around to see them. We wandered around killing time before heading off. Our bed that night would be in the youth hostel at Strathpeffer.

We only used the hostel there that one time. Strathpeffer, once famous as a Victorian spa resort, was a place out of time. Still busy as a centre for coach tours, with many imposing hotels, it had an air of quiet neglect. The HF once had a house there, using the area for walking holidays, and that was at a time when the road system was poorer than today. The hostel we had to ourselves and so we had a quiet night. Next morning we just got up and left. As we drove through the Black Isle and over the Kessock bridge we decided that rather than drive down the A9 we would go another route down the east side of the Great Glen through Foyers to look at the falls there. Although the run was fine the waterfalls proved disappointing due to the lack of water. The rest of the way home took us through Fort William, then Altshellach HF house where we stopped by for tea provided by my friend John, the manager there. As we drove up towards the moor of Rannoch, the oil warning light began to blink furiously. Thinking again that we had a serious problem I decided to pull into a lay-by and walk back to find a telephone. The nearest was way back at the Glencoe ski centre, so it looked like a fair walk. But we were in luck. We had only walked a few hundred yards when a car pulled up to ask what the trouble was. Using their mobile phone I was able to contact the Automobile Association and within an hour a breakdown vehicle had arrived. It seemed that the problem was only minor and soon we were on our way home.

The Corbetts

AFTER BOTH RAB AND I completed our Munros I just kept on going to the hills. For a while even Rab had fallen by the wayside. Many of our peers who also completed the Munros soon gave up going to the hills altogether. For some, age and failing fitness were reason enough to sit back on well-earned laurels. Others, however, did them all over again – when we heard of this we began to wonder what sort of a job they did of them the first time round – and some people just disappeared. Although I did many Munros over again I still only climbed many just the one time. While we kept going out together on various walks that often linked some of our big outings, I found being an HF leader was an excellent way to maintain my interest in the mountains. I made many friends and met people from all over the world. From about 1993 onwards we did fewer and fewer Munros until Rab eventually stopped climbing them altogether. A new challenge eventually took us both to the hills as a team: climbing the next highest hills in Scotland, the Corbetts. The realisation did not just happen overnight, for in our early days we had been climbing Corbetts almost as long as we climbed the bigger Munros. Hills such as Ben Arthur, or the Brack and Ben Donich, we visited many times.

As we worked our way around the Corbetts we found ourselves rediscovering places we had not been to for years. Glen Etive was a particular example of an area we drove past for a long time after we had climbed all its Munros. The glen provided us with some memorable days, such as the day in early June when we climbed Beinn Mhic Chasgaig. This is certainly a difficult hill just to gain access to: a bridge over the river Etive has a locked gate and barbed wire, and the only way over is to wade across the river at a shallow point, something that is not always possible. However, once across you find yourself in an area that has been described as Himalayan, a most appropriate description on the day we climbed the hill. We soon found ourselves in among steep-sided valleys. We reached a point where we would have to ascend the mountain either up a steep rough gorge or up the side of it. We chose to climb keeping to the left side of the gorge and were soon struggling in intense heat up the heather slopes and eventually onto the ridge. As Rab and I wandered along the top of the hill we found many different varieties of mountain flowers. It was quite unusual to see such a profusion of flowers in bloom at the same time and in the one small area.

As we climbed, the views began to open up all around us and we found ourselves looking at many familiar Munros from an angle we had never seen them before. Under the strong sun our progress was slow. Rab had on his panama hat to ward off the sun and looked every bit the eccentric that he is. Just as we came up to the summit cairn we noticed a couple of people a little way off the top and in no apparent hurry to get there. I thought that this was odd behaviour as most people climb hills to reach the top. As we sat eating our lunch they eventually wandered over to where we were sitting. An elderly couple, they did not look like hillwalkers, more like birdwatchers, I thought, with their beanie sun hats, binoculars and notebooks. When he reached us the wee bloke says to me quite excitedly, 'I've just seen a painted lady!' Without batting an eyelid I replied, 'Aye, an ah've jist seen a rid admiral right behind ye' – and sure enough there on the cairn fluttering in the breeze was a red admiral butterfly. The wee man was pretty well taken aback: he obviously took us for a pair of hairy-arsed hillwalkers, thinking we wouldn't recognise a butterfly if we saw one. It seemed that they were part of a group of people doing a survey on the extent of butterflies, and they were obviously pleased to meet walkers with interests other than kicking cairns. Rab and myself took our leave and descended the bealach which continues on up onto Clachlet and Meall a'Bhuird. But our route was down again into Glen Etive where, instead of walking back to where we had crossed the river, we simply waded over and walked along the road back to the car.

On another Corbett trip at the beginning of May in 1996 we left Glasgow at midday, an unusually late start for us. Our destination was the tiny hamlet of Ardeonaig on the south side of Loch Tay. It was not a very inspiring day; wet, cold and thoroughly miserable. For a long time we sat in the car debating what to do till eventually we decided to make the effort. As the old saying has it, 'Always set off for your hill.' Our route was up into the narrow defile of the Finglen burn. As Rab and I walked up the glen we were struck by a sense of dereliction, a strong feeling that the glen, haunted by the plaintive call of a lone curlew, had been left to waste away. Just beyond an area of ruined shielings we came upon a large area of bog which was littered with the rotting carcasses of many sheep and lambs. Only as we reached the bealach did we see some signs of wildlife: a few poor-looking deer hinds and grouse. It was now time to climb up onto our hill, Creag Uchdag, but first we had lunch, hunched down out of the cold wind in a large peat hag.

Now togged up with all our extra clothes and skins we ascended into the mist and soon were ploughing knee-deep in snow. Cresting the ridge we were assailed by a biting easterly wind in our faces. Working on a compass bearing, we plodded around the many false tops and bumps till we eventually hit the summit trig point. It was becoming too much of a whiteout to linger here at all. So with a quick bearing I headed us off the hill, firstly north along the ridge to a point just before Meall nan Oighreag and then into the glen we came up. I think both of us were glad to leave this glen behind – it was one of the sourest places we had ever been to. Once back at the car we changed quickly and sped off to the youth hostel at Killin to spend a night. It had been many years since we had last stayed at Killin and we were pleased to receive a warm welcome and find the place reasonably quiet.

The forecast being more promising, the next day we headed east along the north side of Loch Tay to turn off up through Fortingall then Coshieville and up the road towards Tummel Bridge. Our hills this time were Meall Tairneachan and Farragon Hill. We parked at Tomphubil in a small car park near an old lime kiln. This was about as near as we could get to these hills. Our climbing was starting about 400 metres above sea level. We could have used a road a little farther north but opted to keep away and follow our own route. This took us up the side of a large area of forestry with an old drystane wall in places beside it. Beyond the tree line we just walked over the tops till we reached our first trig point. Here we had lunch sitting in the warm sun, so different from the previous day. These hills were teeming with dozens of mountain hare. There were plenty of red deer around too, as well as groups of ptarmigan and grouse. To the west rose the peak of Schiehallion and Loch Tummel lay to the north. As we continued east we came onto a road and on rounding a bend found ourselves in an extensive area of mine workings. There were buildings, machinery and piles of spoil everywhere and at one place we looked into a tunnel running straight into the hillside. We had to keep moving off the road out of the way of large trucks carrying away some sort of ore. We were passing through a barytes mine. I remember seeing barytes mines marked on maps of the north end of Arran. The clay-like ore was being used as some sort of lubricant in drilling for oil in the North Sea. Bashing on past this noise and mess, we skirted the hill of Creagan Lochan on a grassy track contouring around the hill then dropping to a burn running from Lochan Lairig Laoigh. Here we had another break. From now on there was no definite path for our ascent of the Farragon Hill. From the Farragon we retraced our steps past the mines and kept to the road for about a half mile beyond our first hill where we turned off to strike a line at the corner of the forestry where we had started, back down to the lime kiln.

Of all the Corbetts we climbed I still feel that the toughest ones are to be found in the West Highlands. Our first forays there took us in and out of Glen Cona and Glen Scaddle to visit Resourie bothy. In the same area we found ourselves on the icy summit of Beinn a'Chearchill with no ice-axes or crampons, asking ourselves what the hell we were doing there just to top a Corbett. On a midsummer weekend in 1996 we set off to hammer as many as we could in the Glenfinnan and Arisaig area. It turned out that we were the ones who suffered. After a wet night sleeping in the car we set off about four in the morning to spend a long misty day climbing the three Corbetts of Rois-Bheinn, Sgurr na Ba Glaise and An Stuc. Our early start was rewarded with a stunning West Highland evening which we were too tired to appreciate fully. Another bad night in the car saw us fit only for what we thought was an easy hill. As usual we were totally wrong: the mountain we climbed that day proved to be one of the most interesting we had climbed in years. As we pulled ourselves wearily onto the summit of this hill Rab became very excited. By pure chance we had stumbled onto a hill at the right time of year and had found in a small area of about half an acre one of the rarest mountain flowers in the country, diapensia lapponica, an alpine flower discovered by accident by an English botanist in 1953.

'Keep shouting!'

WE MADE A LONG-OVERDUE return to the misty island of Skye, Rab, myself and wee Billy Billings, to attempt to walk the length of the 'Escarpment,' an undulating ridge running almost from Portree to Duntulm. A long drive from Yoker took us to the tiny youth hostel overlooking Uig bay. Our plan was to walk this ridge that forms the backbone of the Trotternish peninsula. Uig hostel is splendidly situated, and when we arrived we were well pleased to find that it was practically empty. When we awoke the next morning Rab and I had both spent a bad night. Our eyes were streaming and the dormitory was stinking like a football changing room. It seemed that Wullie had been up during the night, liberally applying his evil-smelling Olbas liniment (or, as we called it, Ould Bass). Straight away Rab confiscated what was left and that wasn't much. We then banished him to the farthest-away corner of the room.

Our walk that morning took us up the south side of Glen Uig itself. Walking up the road we passed a house where a man was working in his garden and a taxi was sitting in the driveway. Acting on impulse we enquired if it would be possible for him to pick us up at the north end of the ridge. This was fine by him and we arranged to phone him later on. Moving on, we began to pass on our right strange rock shapes reminiscent of China or Vietnam. Once beyond this surreal landscape we were soon out on a more familiar terrain of open moorland. At this point Billy began to trail behind: he was obviously not fit for the hills. With such a slow pace, if we let him he would dictate the day's walk. When the path finally fizzled out we walked directly towards the escarpment at the Bealach a'Mhoramhain, with Billy straggling at the rear.

From here you look down and over the eastern side of the peninsula. Our route from here was north over the top of Ben Edra at 611 metres. There was initially some mist on Ben Edra and when I reached the top I sat waiting, listening to Rab who was chastising Billy as he waited for him to come up. It was a classic example of 'Keep shouting as long as ah can hear ye.' After a short breather we set off. Rab had by now decided to send Billy off at the next bealach. At first he was reluctant to keep going but Rab had strong words with him and when he caught up with me said, 'Ah sent him aff wi his lip tremlin.'

With Wullie red-carded and sent off we could now make good progress along the undulating escarpment. The going was unusually wet under foot, but the sun was shining so who could complain? A short climb brought us up to Bioda Buidhe which overlooks strange finger-like pinnacles. The ridge here is broken and steep – at one place we were forced to detour away from a deep indentation in the cliff face. Beyond here, however, the path drops down to meet the road that runs from Uig to Staffin. Here we had a pleasant drum-up before continuing northwards again.

As Rab and I wound our way along the faint path we found ourselves looking down from Meall na Suiramach into the strange landscape that is the Quirang unfolding below us. We wandered along the top of the ridge, looking down at the Prison, the Needles, the Quirang and the Tables. Near this last part of our walk the ridge or escarpment divides. Our route now took us along the main ridge to Sgurr Mor from where we descended long heather-clad slopes towards the Kilmaluag river and the small hamlet of Connista, from where we walked out to the main road and turned west to Duntlum where there was a telephone. We phoned the taxi driver, thus ending a superb walk on the north end of the Trotternish escarpment.

The next day we set off for home but decided to take the long way and include a walk up into the Quirang itself. After a short drive along the minor road that cuts across the escarpment from Uig to Staffin, we parked the car where the road drops from a cleft in the ridge. A pleasant wander took us among this peculiar landscape which seemed to change at every turn. We returned to the car and drove down the coast, stopping briefly to view the Kilt Rock. Our next port of call was a walk up to see the Storr and the weird pinnacle of the Old Man of Storr. This outlandish monolith – from afar and up close – looked unclimbable, but it had in fact first been scaled by the English climber Don Whillans as recently as 1966. Our visit to the misty isle was now at an end. We had only traversed the north end of the escarpment, probably the best part, but it still left a feeling of unfinished business.

The Rolling Hills o' the Borders

OUR FIRST VISIT TO THE Galloway Hills was at the end of March 1994. It was a strange feeling to be heading south in order to climb hills. Ayrshire is a county of contrasts. Although it is mainly agricultural, we were soon passing through many small villages that owed their existence to coal mining. Most were very run down and shabby looking. One such village was that of Patna. In an area littered with the detritus of a long-dead industry, it was eerie to see the smoke of coal fires rising from almost every chimney in sight as the sun burned away the early morning mist.

Our first hill that day, to the south-east of the village of Dalmellington, was the lone Corbett, Cairnsmore of Carsphairn, which lies to the north of the main group of the Galloway hills. We parked at a place called The Green Well of Scotland. Our route for a short distance followed the east side of the Water of Deugh. We then followed a track, through fields full of black cattle, which contoured up the hillside. When the track came to an end we followed a large drystane wall almost straight to our summit cairn. From the top we were rewarded with good views of our next hills to the south, while to the north we could see the Kilpatrick hills above Clydebank and the Clyde valley. We were also in a good position to see most of the country through which the Southern Upland Way passes. To the west lay the Firth of Clyde with the peaks of Arran in the distance and the huge lump of Ailsa Craig much closer. Our descent was south then west along the rolling grassy slopes of the Black Shoulder, Dunool and Willeanna and on to rejoin the track near to the Water of Deugh.

Back at the car we quickly changed the boots and drove the short distance to the Carsphairn Inn, where we enjoyed an excellent pub lunch before driving on to the Minnigaff youth hostel near Newton Stewart. As usual we had the hostel to ourselves. The warden and his wife enthused about the refurbishment just completed in the kitchens. Unfortunately this did not extend to the dormitories which were cold and bleak-looking. We had a quiet night and early next morning saw us off up the Girvan road, heading for Glen Trool. We parked near Bruce's Stone and on a dreary-looking morning set off into the wilds of the Galloway Hills, following up the Buchan burn. Our hill for the day was the Merrick. After about a mile or so, as we were beginning to boil in our waterproofs, we reached the bothy at Culsharg. Here we had our first welcome break and the only one under cover till we returned later.

From Culsharg we climbed steadily up through forestry tracks and eventually emerged onto the lower slopes of Benyellary at 719 metres. The weather had by now taken a turn for the worse: it was snowing heavily and visibility was almost nil. In these conditions the sensible thing would have been to turn around and get off. However, there was a wall running in the direction of the Merrick out along the ridge called Neive of the Spit so, rightly or wrongly, on we went, keeping close to it. In time, the dubious shelter afforded by this ruined wall came to nothing as it wandered off in the wrong direction for us, but by now we were committed. Taking a bearing, we plodded on into the teeth of the gale. I struggled along trying to see the compass which I held in frozen fingers (I had forgotten my gloves). My glasses were trapping the driving snow, almost blinding me. But with Rab hanging on to my pack to hold us upright in the wind we soon found ourselves on the top of the hill, though we could not find the trig point. At last there was a slight rise in the ground ahead and there it was, sat in a small hollow. With no stones around or any cairn to afford shelter we quickly took a bearing for our way off and had a hot drink before retreating with the wind now behind us.

A quiet night was had in the hostel that night as we thawed out and dried our gear in preparation for the next day's hill: Corserine. For this walk we parked near Forest Lodge, on an estate with Norwegian owners (part of the Christian Salvesen group, I believe). As we set off through the forestry to the hills we came upon a huge figure of a Black Watch soldier in full dress uniform – the figurehead from a ship sunk by the German invasion of Norway in 1940. We were taking an indirect route onto Corserine rather than the usual cairn-kickers' straight-up-and-down. Firstly we bore south-west through forestry to emerge on to the slopes of Meikle Lump with a climb up onto Meikle Millyea at 740 metres. From here we moved north along the Rhinns of Kells taking in the tops of Milldown and Millfire and then on to Corserine itself. The summit of Corserine was rounded and bare and visibility was much better than the previous day. The Merrick was clear, with no hint of the foul day we had experienced on its top. Although dry, it was bitterly cold and we had on all the gear we had with us, so we did not linger too long before turning along the ridge to North Garry Top and plunging

The salvaged Black Watch figurehead

into the shelter of forestry again. Soon we passed Loch Harrow – a forlorn pair of mallard out in the middle – and after a short walk beside the Polharrow burn we were back at the car.

The next day being wet and very cloudy we opted for a low-level walk by Loch Trool along part of the Southern Upland Way as far as the White Laggan bothy where we had a tea stop. The bothies we visited in this area were more grubby than many we went to in the north, possibly because they were near to the Upland Way walk or handy for mountain-bikers and fishermen. From here we retraced our steps and at Loch Trool we walked along the southern shore and back to the car.

On 18 July we returned to the Galloway Hills. Early on a stunning morning Rab and I went round to pick up Billy Billings at his house. As we pounded on his door it became obvious that he was not at home. Despite severe warnings he had gone off to the town the previous night and had not come home. Sod it, we would just leave the little bugger. So off we went, heading for the braw Galloway hills. We were in for a very hot summer's day. Our hill for the day would be our last Corbett in Galloway, Shalloch on Minnoch. From the car park at Laglanny we set off on the usual forestry track, heading east with our hill in sight ahead. Almost from the start things began to go wrong. It was the usual story of not getting the route right at the beginning. We found that we were in a forest ride but could not get onto the open hillside through the dense trees. Eventually we gave up and retreated almost to the start line, where we then set off once more on the correct track. By now it was very hot. The sun was high in the sky and when we cleared the tree line onto open hillside we were immediately set upon by millions of flies. I have never seen anything like this before or since. Whether it is something that occurs just in the Border hills I don't know. For the whole day we were plagued by hordes of these flies. You could clap your hands and they would be black with them. They settled on your face, hair, eyes, mouth, nose and ears. They were inside our shirts. Rab had on a baseball cap which was full of buzzing flies getting in at the space at the back of his head. In the end I took off my shirt and wrapped it around my head and face.

Shalloch on Minnoch was not a hard Corbett to climb but on that hot summer's day as we sweated up its heather slopes and battled against the flies we felt we were in purgatory. On the summit there was no respite as we turned south along the ridge of the Nick of Carlach and over the top of Tarfessock. Demented, we wandered along the ridge, unable to stop to eat or drink, to the top of Kirriereoch hill. We could have turned off here but decided that the map would look better if the walk were linked to the top of the Merrick, so on we plodded. This visit to the Merrick was in stark contrast to our previous visit a few months earlier. It was now time for the Lords of the Flies to leave. Our hands and arm blackened with squashed flies, and having swallowed enough of them to take off ourselves, we about-turned and returned to Kirriereoch for the descent along the west ridge down to Cross Burn bothy. From here we entered the forestry again with a welcome departure of our flies and found we now had a hard road to walk out. We were hot and dusty with some road-walking before us, but the day had a sting in the tail yet awaiting us. As we approached the Water of Minnoch I realised that the map was marked with a ford at the river. A river it sure was. The ford was wide and too deep for us and although we found a rocky part we still had to strip off to cross. Despite it being high summer and one of the hottest days, the water was freezing. Once across, we did the last few miles along the hard tarmac in weary silence. The Galloway Hills were some of the hardest-earned hills that we ever climbed.

A Daunder by Dalnaspidal

A DAUNDER IN THE HILLS at Drumochter was a daunting prospect as Rab and I drove slowly north through mist and fog up the A9. By the time we arrived at Dalnaspidal and parked near the disused station, conditions were no better: all of the Drumochter hills were completely hidden in mist. Our walk for the day began by crossing the railway and onto the old right of way that goes through to Kinnloch Rannoch. The area here, with some poor farming and surrounded by mountains, is mainly wet and boggy. But within a very short distance we saw numerous birds: plover, oystercatcher, wagtail, dipper, wheatear, heron, hawk, mallard, merganser, teal, curlew – this apparently barren landscape was alive with bird life.

After crossing two bridges over the River Garry where it drains from Loch Garry, we were soon ploughing through deep heather up the slopes of our first hill, Meall na Leitreach. As it was so misty we were working by compass from the start. However, as we ascended the slopes we came upon a track running up the hill: we decided to follow it since it was heading on the same bearing as us. Once on the summit, which was fairly level and still on a track in places, we reached the point when you know that the top must be nearby. Telling Rab to stay on the track I walked back at an angle until I came upon the summit cairn and shouted Rab over. At the cairn I attempted to take a bearing for our way off the ridge without being too close to its edge. As we set off I walked onto what I thought was the right way but Rab insisted we take our leave from the cairn. This proved to be a serious error: as the navigator I should have insisted we go off my way.

What we in fact did was to set off in the correct direction but several hundred yards parallel to the route intended. This made us drop straight off the hill in a way that had us contouring along rounded knolls running off the ridge. I had no alternative but to march on regardless, holding as near to the bearing as possible.

The new glasses I was wearing, being plastic lenses, steamed up badly, obscuring my vision and making it difficult to navigate. After a good hour and a half the terrain began to level out and became extremely boggy. This seriously disorientated us. On a really wet boggy stretch we came upon an old boundary fence. As this did not appear on the map we decided to rest, eat something and have a think. At this point we were in danger of tiring ourselves out and becoming totally lost. The could mean the prospect of a night out on the hills with no extra gear or shelter in an area devoid of even dry ground. On looking at the map we decided that the best course would be to head directly west where at some point we were bound to hit a road running north to south.

As we turned onto a westerly bearing the terrain became difficult to negotiate with huge peat hags all around. On our left we could see the ground climb steeply, indicating a hill rising into the mist. We began to realise that we were actually below Creag a'Mhadaidh (612 metres). Although on the right bearing we had overshot where we should have turned west and had come down at the east edge of a large area of peat hags and bog. Soon we could see our road contouring along the side of the hill before us. With great relief we turned and climbed up onto it and we were soon striding along and talking optimistically of continuing with our plan to tackle Beinn Mholach. We decided to walk on to a building marked on the map: if we could shelter there we would decide whether to go for the hill. Looming out of the mist, a fair-sized building began to take shape. This was Duinish: it proved to be a substantial bothy owned by the estate but it had been badly vandalised and its future was in doubt. Once inside and out of the weather we got some wet things off and consumed the last of our tea along with some fruit cake.

Well refreshed and with our spirits revived we decided to have a go at climbing Mholach. After all, it was only two-thirty and there were only 400 or so metres of climbing. From the bothy we set off right on our bearing straight up the hill. Well up the hill we came upon a track which was again going our way so we stuck with this to the summit plateau where it disappeared near some marker cairns. The top part of Mholach is a jumble of rocky tops, each one looking higher in the mist than others.

Eventually I started to zigzag left and right across the hill, coming back onto the correct bearing each time and trying to keep to the middle high ground along the ridge. At last we came to a point with a circle of stones. We took it for the top as I took a wide sweep in the mist, only to find the ground dropping away all round. This was all we could do to ensure that we had reached the summit. Retracing the route we kept to the right edge: this meant that we had circled round the top of the hill.

Following the back bearing the terrain looked totally different: this is not unusual in misty conditions, but there was nothing we could recognise. From out of the mist we could hear the plaintive cry of plovers – we had heard the birds in the mist on the way up and wondered if these were the same birds and whether it was possible they had not moved far. We came upon a piece of water and I was looking at the map, thinking it may be marked, when Rab shouted that we were back on the track we had followed up. Walking down this I was surprised to see that it followed exactly the same bearing we came up. As we got to the road we saw that the track started a few feet from where we had set off up the hill. We had walked a few feet from it right up to the ridge.

Returning to Duinish bothy we found that it had taken us two and a half hours to climb the hill. A short rest and a drink of the remaining fruit juice saw us ready to trudge our way out to Dalnaspidal. Just then we saw a huge flock of greylag geese fly in to settle on the wetlands in front of the bothy – there must have been a good hundred or so birds. Back on the road, by now chilled, quite damp and very weary, we set off to walk out. The road swung away from the flat wet area and came to a substantial bridge over a fast-flowing wild burn. As we crossed over we were dismayed to see the track peter out into the bogs. We could only head towards the river and follow it to the loch to pick up the road where it started further on. This was hard going: by now we were undoubtedly very tired and the wet, rough ground was no help. Nearing the loch we began to see large groups of red deer, a good mixture of stags and hinds, all wearing dull grey coats.

On reaching the road we were relieved to find it was not too rough to walk on and settled down for a long, slow, painful walk. Although knackered we could still joke at the way things were feeling: pain meant you were still alive and that's what mattered. Here we were, in the middle of the braw heilands on such a day. It had been misty and dull, but what atmosphere! All around were myriads of birds and the hillsides were alive with hundreds of deer. At the end of Loch Garry we completed the circle and found ourselves back in the wet area near Dalnaspidal still teeming with birds. At the car we changed quickly. The light was fading and we sped off south for about ten miles to the turn-off to Struan, where we had had lunch in the hotel on a previous trip. Beside the hotel is a small caravan site where we put up the big Vango tent that gave us plenty of room to sit around under cover. With Rab struggling to blow up the airbed I got the stove going and the dinner on. Our meal of rice mixed with sauces was washed down with our by now customary glass of red wine.

Next morning as we took down the tent I was reading up the guidebook and looking at the maps when it dawned on me that we had missed the real summit of Ben Mholach. There is in fact a large cairn and a trig point on the top. We saw neither so it was two dejected wee men who drove home in gloomy silence that morning.

Three weeks later we returned to the same hill. On a bright, sunny summer's day we climbed Ben Mholach from its south side, from Annat on Loch Rannoch. Once on the true summit, reached after a long, hot, dusty slog, we could see that there was indeed a series of false tops which we had followed in the mist. What we had mistaken for the summit was about 200 feet lower and about a quarter of a mile away.

Faraway Hills are Still as Green

WITH THE DAWNING OF A new millennium it became clear as the year wore on that Rab Doyle, my old comrade and partner of so many great hillwalking days, had sadly decided to retire from the hills. At the age of seventy-five, time and the pursuit of women had taken their inevitable toll. Rab used to talk of wee Stukky adopting the 'foetal poseetion' and turning his face to the wall: now it seemed that he himself was adopting the 'missionary poseetion'. Given the choice Rab would now rather chase women than go to his once beloved hills. With a great feeling of loss I was left to carry on climbing the Corbetts on my own. Although unspoken, Rab and I knew it would happen sooner or later, although not quite as soon as I had expected. Despite being able enough for the hills, Rab had, I think, looked at wee Bill – now eighty-six and with a recently broken pelvis – and had decided to quit with dignity rather than soldier on to the bitter end like so many others. My dilemma was, should I continue going to the hills or just call it a day and retire gracefully? After all, I have had a long run at the hills, having begun my hillwalking at an earlier age than most of my contemporaries. Well, I was the last of the old gang and still fit and able, but it meant going on alone. Actually, just going to the hills was easy, but to continue without the company of my old pal was the most difficult thing of all. There was no option: I would have to test myself and, as I said so often to others, 'just set off for my hills'.

I had selected the remote Corbett of Stob an Aonaich Mhoir on the east side of Loch Ericht. Now here I was, without the old yin in the passenger seat, driving north up the A9 on my own. It was certainly a strange feeling, heading for the hills with only the radio for company. Why was I doing this? It would not be just another day on a new hill: it would be a quest to find whether I had the bottle to continue going to the hills on my own. Although the morning was bright and sunny as I left the city, the forecast was not promising. The old adage came to mind of 'Bright too soon, rain before noon'. All too soon I found myself at the west end of Loch Rannoch, looking for somewhere to park. A large lay-by caught my attention and I remembered that it was where the walk into Ben Alder started. This would be an excellent place to begin as it would connect up previous walks nicely despite adding two miles of walking to the day.

With a quick snack I got ready. As per usual just as you are ready to set off, the rain came on and so I togged up with my skins and set off on foot alongside the loch whose placid oily waters were being skimmed by a few migrant swallows. At the bridge of Ericht I found my road into the hills barred by a high locked gate with all kinds of stalking information. The gate was climbable but right next to a house where I suppose I could have asked permission – but this was something we never ever did in all our years on the hills and I wasn't about to start now. To the right of the gate was a natural wood so I simply walked along the road and up through the trees. This was not a bad start as it got me off the tarmac road, if only for a short time. The wood was quiet with only the sound of my boots snapping the odd twigs and a distant cuckoo calling, maybe mocking me. Once beyond the forest I had to negotiate a high deer fence before continuing on the road. From here on it was a long, slow climb as the road wound its way into the hills. It was an unusual feeling to be plodding along with only your thoughts to keep you going. In the past when on my own I always drove myself on at a hard pace, and today was no exception. With the rain drizzling away I tramped on with the hood up trying to keep off the hard road and sticking to the softer grassy verge. After a good hour's steady going I looked up and was surprised to see a large hydro dam before me. Beyond at a fork in the way stood a fair-sized concrete bridge that looked as if it had recently been rebuilt. This seemed as good a time as any to have my first break so I climbed under the bridge out of the rain and had a hot drink and a bite to eat. I had worked a late shift the previous night and as I huddled there I began to doze off. But sitting under a bridge in the rain was not going to get me my hill, so I got myself going again and pushed on.

One of the most daunting things about a long trek is seeing the road snaking away for miles ahead, and uphill at that, so I looked at the map and decided to have a stop under the next bridge about three miles ahead. The surrounding hills looked bleak and uninviting. A grey, cloudy sky made for poor visibility and as if to emphasise the desolation I passed a gaunt ruin of what once was a decent-sized house. The silence was almost deafening. Apart from me, all I could hear was the whirring of the snipe that I put up occasionally. The next bridge seemed to come up very quickly but the position of the hills didn't seem quite right. On closer inspection of the map I realised that this bridge was not marked, and there was me thinking I was eating up the miles at a tremendous rate. By now I was wet on the outside and soaked on the inside with condensation. The waterproofs I wore were too good so every once in a while when the rain eased I opened my jacket up to cool down. The bit was now firmly between my teeth. My hill was in view and the temptation to turn off the road and go for its ridge was strong. For a while I resisted, knowing that the road was still climbing and every step took it up and nearer to the hill. But eventually I found that the track was almost level and continuing along it was a waste of time, so off I turned and headed towards the ridge.

From experience I knew that the top was probably well out of sight but the route took me up through short grass and heather. This was now becoming a race with the elements. As if on cue the mist began to roll in and the rain became heavier: it was as if the mountains were throwing everything at me to make me turn back. The harder I pushed the faster I began to tire – I needed food. I stopped and sat down with my back to the rain and ate as fast as I could. Peering up the hill I could no longer see any distance in the thickening mist, so to be on the safe side I took a compass bearing: if I had to retreat I would simply take a back bearing the way I came. Zipping up my jacket and tightening the rucksack straps I got going again. The blood was up and I was going for broke. As I breasted the ridge the wind blasted me full in the face. The rain, turning to hailstones and eventually driving snow, lashed me as I fought my way up. One top came, then another, then all of a sudden there it was – a lovely big cairn. As if conceding defeat the snow stopped and I reached the cairn, gasping for breath but jubilant at getting there. With a quick walk on I could see no other point higher and as an afterthought, just to prove it, I got the camera out to take a snap of me at the top. Just then the cloud broke up and as if looking through a torn grey curtain I could see up and down the length of Loch Ericht. Straight across on the opposite side of the loch stood Ben Alder with huge streaks of snow on its top. Below I could see the little bay where the bothy is. I was ecstatic, here in the middle of nowhere and on my own. Suddenly I had a thought: in my pack was a mobile phone which I recently began carrying for emergencies but the thing never always worked. I dialled home and got through to my wife – for the only time that day I didn't feel so isolated.

It was now time to go. With the wind now at my back and visibility improving by the minute I danced off the hill taking a direct line towards the road. As if to see me on my way I was accompanied by the plaintive cry of a lone plover. Looking along the ridge where I had considered taking a short cut I was glad that I had resisted the temptation, for the ridge was wide with countless peat bogs which would have been a difficult approach. With my hill behind me, euphoria sped me on my way but there was still a long distance to go. The hard road began to take its toll on me. Although my stride was still strong the tarmac now made the old feet ache. What seemed to be a continuous uphill on the way in still had little bits to climb and I was now feeling them. Bashing on, I knew that I needed another break for food and drink and to sort my socks which were being pushed into the front of the boots. Once back at the concrete bridge I scrambled underneath out of the wind and rain the best I could and pulled my boots off to let my feet cool down, socks steaming as the sweat dried in the air. On looking at my map I considered making a detour across the dam and heading along the bottom of the loch to join the Ben

Alder track. I quickly dismissed the idea for, although this would have taken me out to where the car was parked, it would add a few extra, hard miles to an already tough day. Time was wearing on, and tiredness was working against me. It was an effort to concentrate and think straight and I had to make a real effort to get moving again. Wearily I laced up my boots and struggled back up onto the road.

It was now only three miles to the road end and yet I was beginning to stagger all over the road. My knees and hips were beginning to ache badly. Rounding a twist in the road I saw the wood where I had started from. Heading straight to the corner of the high deer fence, I clambered over it with surprising ease. Staggering drunkenly up a slight slope I wondered where the hell that climb came from. I gained the wood but I couldn't find the path so to hell with it, I went right through the trees. Emerging the other side I walked through a large field towards the road with several large hares running from my path. The last mile along a metalled road is always the hardest at the end of a long day and I was now on autopilot, plodding wearily through the drizzle. Suddenly I found myself at the lay-by fumbling in pockets for the car keys. Throwing my pack in the boot I scrambled into the back seat and just sat there, too exhausted to even attempt to remove wet gear or boots. I had walked eighteen miles in seven and a half hours and was well pleased with myself. It definitely was no ordinary day on the hills. I had set myself a personal test and had proved to myself that at the end of the day, faraway hills are still as green as they once used to be.

Some other books published by **LUATH** PRESS

Mountain Days & Bothy Nights

Dave Brown and Ian Mitchell

ISBN 0 946487 15 4   PBK   £7.50

Acknowledged as a classic of mountain writing still in demand ten years after its first publication, this book takes you into the bothies, howffs and dosses on the Scottish hills. Fishgut Mac, Desperate Dan and Stumpy the Big Yin stalk hill and public house, evading gamekeepers and Royalty with a camaraderie which was the trademark of Scots hillwalking in the early days.

'*The fun element comes through... how innocent the social polemic seems in our nastier world of today... the book for the rucksack this year.*'
Hamish Brown, SCOTTISH MOUNTAINEERING CLUB JOURNAL

Scotland's Mountains before the Mountaineers

Ian Mitchell

ISBN 0 946487 39 1   PBK £9.99

In this ground-breaking book, Ian Mitchell tells the story of explorations and ascents in the Scottish Highlands in the days before mountaineering became a popular sport – when bandits, Jacobites, poachers and illicit distillers traditionally used the mountains as sanctuary. The book also gives a detailed account of the map makers, road builders, geologists, astrono-mers and naturalists, many of whom ascended hitherto untrodden summits while working in the Scottish Highlands.

Scotland's Mountains before the Mountaineers is divided into four Highland regions, with a map of each region showing key summits. While not designed primarily as a guide, it will be a useful handbook for walkers and climbers. Based on a wealth of new research, this book offers a fresh perspective that will fascinate climbers and mountaineers and everyone interested in the history of mountaineering, cartography, the evolution of landscape and the social history of the Scottish Highlands.

The Highland Geology Trail

John L Roberts

ISBN 0946487 36 7   PBK £5.99

Where can you find the oldest rocks in Europe?
Where can you see ancient hills around 800 million years old?

How do you tell whether a valley was carved out by a glacier, not a river?
What are the Fucoid Beds?
Where do you find rocks folded like putty?
How did great masses of rock pile up like snow in front of a snow-plough?
When did volcanoes spew lava and ash to form Skye, Mull and Rum?
Where can you find fossils on Skye?

'*...a lucid introduction to the geological record in general, a jargon-free exposition of the regional background, and a series of descriptions of specific localities of geological interest on a "trail" around the highlands.*

Having checked out the local references on the ground, I can vouch for their accuracy and look forward to investigating farther afield, informed by this guide.

Great care has been taken to explain specific terms as they occur and, in so doing, John Roberts has created a resource of great value which is eminently usable by anyone with an interest in the outdoors...the best bargain you are likely to get as a geology book in the foreseeable future.'
Jim Johnston, PRESS AND JOURNAL

But n Ben A-Go-Go

Matthew Fitt

ISBN 0 946487 82 0   HB   £10.99
ISBN 1 84282 041 1   PB   £6.99

The year is 2090. Global flooding has left most of Scotland under water. The descendants of those who survived God's Flood live in a community of floating island parishes, known collectively as Port. Port's citizens live in mortal fear of Senga, a supervirus whose victims are kept in a giant hospital warehouse in sealed capsules called Kists. Paolo Broon is a low-ranking cyberjanny. His life-partner, Nadia, lies forgotten and alone in Omega Kist 624 in the Rigo Imbeki Medical Center. When he receives an unexpected message from his radge criminal father to meet him at But n Ben A-Go-Go, Paolo's life is changed forever. He must traverse VINE, Port and the Drylands and deal with rebel American tourists and crabbit Dundonian microchips to discover the truth about his family's past in order to free Nadia from the sair grip of the merciless Senga. Set in a distinctly unbonnie future-Scotland, the novel's dangerous atmosphere and psychologically-malkied characters weave a tale that both chills and intrigues. In But n Ben A-Go-Go Matthew Fitt takes the allegedly dead language of Scots and energises it with a narrative that crackles and fizzes with life.

an entertaining and ground-breaking book EDWIN MORGAN

... if you can't get hold of a copy, mug somebody MARK STEPHEN, SCOTTISH CONNECTION, BBC RADIO SCOTLAND

...the last man who tried anything like this was Hugh MacDiarmid MICHAEL FRY, TODAY PROGRAMME, BBC RADIO 4

Bursting with sly humour, staggeringly imaginative, often poignant and at times exploding with Uzi-blazing action, this book is a cracker... With Matthew Fitt's book I began to think and sometimes dream in Scots. GREGOR STEELE, TIMES EDUCATIONAL SUPPLEMENT

On the Trail of Queen Victoria in the Highlands

Ian R. Mitchell

UK ISBN 0 946487 79 0 PBK £7.99

How many Munros did Queen Victoria bag?

What 'essential services' did John Brown perform for Victoria?

(and why was Albert always tired?)

How many horses (to the nearest hundred) were needed to undertake a Royal Tour?

What happens when you send a republican on the tracks of Queen Victoria in the Highlands? a.. you get a book somewhat more interesting than the usual run of the mill royalist biographies!

Ian R. Mitchell took up the challenge of attempting to write with critical empathy on the peregrinations of Vikki Regina in the Highlands, and about her residence at Balmoral, through which a neo-feudal fairyland was created on Upper Deeside. The expeditions, social rituals and iconography of that world are explored and exploded from within, in what Mitchell terms a Bolshevisation of Balmorality. He follows in Victoria's footsteps throughout the Cairngorms and beyond, to the further reaches of the Highlands. On this journey, a grudging respect and even affection for Vikki ('the best of the bunch') emerges.

The book is designed to enable the armchair/motorised reader, or walker, to follow in the steps of the most widely-travelled royal personage in the Highlands since Bonnie Prince Charlie had wandered there a century earlier.

Index map and 12 detailed maps
21 walks in Victoria's footsteps
Rarely seen Washington Wilson photographs
Colour and black and white reproductions of contemporary paintings

On the Trail of Queen Victoria in the Highlands will also appeal to those with an interest in the social and cultural history of Scotland and the Highlands - and the author, ever-mindful of his own 'royalties', hopes the declining band of monarchists might also be persuaded to give the book a try.

The Supernatural Highlands

Francis Thompson

ISBN 0 946487 31 6 PBK £8.99

An authoritative exploration of the otherworld of the Highlander, happenings and beings hitherto thought to be outwith the ordinary forces of nature. A simple introduction to the way of life of rural Highland and Island communities, this new edition weaves a path through second sight, the evil eye, witchcraft, ghosts, fairies and other supernatural beings, offering new sight-lines on areas of belief once dismissed as folklore and superstition.

The Joy of Hillwalking

Ralph Storer

ISBN 0 946487 28 6 PBK £7.50

Apart, perhaps, from the joy of sex, the joy of hillwalking brings more pleasure to more people than any other form of human activity.

'Alps, America, Scandinavia, you name it – Storer's been there, so why the hell shouldn't he bring all these various and varied places into his observations... [He] even admits to losing his virginity after a day on the Aggy Ridge... Well worth its place alongside Storer's earlier works.' TAC

The Hydro Boys: Pioneers of Renewable Energy

Emma Wood

ISBN 1 84282 047 8 PB £8.99

The hydro-electric project was a crusade, with a marvellous goal: the prize of affordable power for all from Scottish rainfall

This book is a journey through time, and across

and beneath the Highland landscape...it is not just a story of technology and politics but of people.

I heard about drowned farms and hamlets, the ruination of the salmon-fishing and how Inverness might be washed away if the dams failed inland. I was told about the huge veins of crystal they found when they were tunnelling deep under the mountains and when I wanted to know who 'they' were: what stories I got in reply! I heard about Poles, Czechs, poverty-stricken Irish, German spies, intrepid locals and the heavy drinking, fighting and gambling which went on in the NoSHEB contractors' camps. EMMA WOOD

Nobody should forget the human sacrifice made by those who built the dams all those years ago. The politicians, engineers and navvies of the era bequeathed to us the major source of renewable energy down to the present day. Their legacy will continue to serve us far into the 21st century.

BRIAN WILSON MP, Energy Minister, announcing a 'new deal for hydro' which now 'provides 50 per cent of the UK's renewable energy output. the largest generator serves more than 4 million customers.' THE SCOTSMAN

Red Sky at Night
John Barrington
ISBN 0 946487 60 X PB £8.99

John Barrington is a shepherd to over 750 Blackface ewes who graze 2,000 acres of some of Britain's most beautiful hills overlooking the deep dark water of Loch Katrine in Perthshire. The yearly round of lambing, dipping, shearing and the sales is marvellously interwoven into the story of the glen, of Rob Roy in whose house John now lives, of curling when the ice is thick enough, and of sheep dog trials in the summer. Whether up to the hills or along the glen, John knows the haunts of the local wildlife: the wily hill fox, the grunting badger, the herds of red deer, and the shrews, voles and insects which scurry underfoot. He sets his seasonal clock by the passage of birds on the loch, and jealously guards over the golden eagle's eyrie in the hills. Paul Armstrong's sensitive illustrations are the perfect accompaniment to the evocative text.

Mr Barrington is a great pleasure to read. One learns more things about the countryside from this account of one year than from a decade of 'The Archers'.
THE DAILY TELEGRAPH

Powerful and evocative... a book which brings vividly to life the landscape, the wildlife, the farm animals and the people who inhabit John's vista. He makes it easy for the reader to fall in love with both his surrounds and his commune with nature.
THE SCOTTISH FIELD

An excellent and informative book.... not only an account of a shepherd's year but also the diary of a naturalist. Little escapes Barrington's enquiring eye and, besides the life cycle of a sheep, he also gives those of every bird, beast, insect and plant that crosses his path, mixing their histories with descriptions of the geography, local history and folklore of his surroundings.
TLS

The family life at Glengyle is wholesome, appealing and not without a touch of the Good Life. Many will envy Mr Barrington his fastness home as they cruise up Loch Katrine on the tourist steamer.
THE FIELD

The Road Dance
John MacKay
ISBN 1 84282 040 0 PB £6.99

Why would a young woman, dreaming of a new life in America, sacrifice all and commit an act so terrible that she severs all hope of happiness again?

Life in the Scottish Hebrides can be harsh – 'The Edge of the World' some call it. For Kirsty MacLeod, the love of Murdo and their dreams of America promise an escape from the scrape of the land, the suppression of the church and the inevitability of the path their lives would take.

But the Great War looms Murdo is conscripted. The villagers hold a grand Road Dance to send their young men off to battle. As the dancers swirl and sup, the wheels of tragedy are set in motion.

[MacKay] has captured time, place and atmosphere superbly... a very good debut
MEG HENDERSON

Powerful, shocking, heartbreaking...
DAILY MAIL

With a gripping plot that subtly twists and turns, vivid characterisation and a real sense of time and tradition, this is an absorbing, powerful first novel. The impression it made on me will remain for some time.
THE SCOTS MAGAZINE

Luath Press Limited

committed to publishing well written books worth reading

LUATH PRESS takes its name from Robert Burns, whose little collie Luath (*Gael.*, swift or nimble) tripped up Jean Armour at a wedding and gave him the chance to speak to the woman who was to be his wife and the abiding love of his life. Burns called one of *The Twa Dogs* Luath after Cuchullin's hunting dog in *Ossian's Fingal*. Luath Press was established in 1981 in the heart of Burns country, and is now based a few steps up the road from Burns' first lodgings on Edinburgh's Royal Mile.
Luath offers you distinctive writing with a hint of unexpected pleasures.

Most bookshops in the UK, the US, Canada, Australia, New Zealand and parts of Europe either carry our books in stock or can order them for you. To order direct from us, please send a £sterling cheque, postal order, international money order or your credit card details (number, address of cardholder and expiry date) to us at the address below. Please add post and packing as follows: UK – £1.00 per delivery address; overseas surface mail – £2.50 per delivery address; overseas airmail – £3.50 for the first book to each delivery address, plus £1.00 for each additional book by airmail to the same address. If your order is a gift, we will happily enclose your card or message at no extra charge.

Luath Press Limited
543/2 Castlehill
The Royal Mile
Edinburgh EH1 2ND
Scotland
Telephone: 0131 225 4326 (24 hours)
Fax: 0131 225 4324
email: gavin.macdougall@luath.co.uk
Website: www.luath.co.uk